Angels of Darkness

ANGELS

OF DARKNESS

Dramatic Effect in Samuel Beckett
with Special Reference to
Eugène Ionesco

by Colin Duckworth

New York · Barnes & Noble Books
(a division of Harper & Row Publishers, Inc.)

ISBN 06 4917878

Published in the U.S.A. 1972 by
HARPER & ROW PUBLISHERS, INC.
BARNES & NOBLE IMPORT DIVISION

Printed in Great Britain
in 11 point Baskerville type
by Unwin Brothers Limited
Woking and London

To
Mary, Tessa, and Mark
for whom Beckett must
now seem a way of life

Acknowledgements

My thanks are due to the following:

Peter James and the management and staff of the Young Vic; Peter O'Toole and the management and staff of the Nottingham Playhouse. But for their help and patience the survey of audience response to *Waiting for Godot* and *Endgame* would not have been possible. To those who took the trouble to complete and return the questionnaires I am also very grateful.

Dr James Knowlson was kind enough to invite me to lecture at the Samuel Beckett Exhibition when it opened at Reading in May 1971, and that lecture grew into Chapter 4.

I am very grateful to Martin Esslin and Professor Ruby Cohn for reading the book in typescript and making several judicious comments. For the book's shortcomings I alone am responsible, of course.

Mrs M. C. Bond battled resolutely with my handwriting and with percentages.

Contents

page

INTRODUCTION

Illumination by comparison: why Beckett and Ionesco? – The function and effect of dramatic structures – *Godot* and audiences in the 1950s – Interviews with Beckett – Forms of imprisonment: San Quentin and the Universe   13

I THE MORTAL COIL

The problem of mortality, as treated by Beckett, Ionesco, and other dramatists – Contrasting attitudes to birth – Empathic transmission of anguish leading to Heidegger or Pascal   23

2 EXPLORATION AND RESPONSE

The exploration of an 'unusable' zone (Beckett) – Problems of dramatising private fantasies – The trap of psychocriticism (degrading and backward-looking) – The reciprocal interrogation between drama and spectator – The play unperformed: its aesthetic status nil – Ambiguous theatricality of *Endgame* – Actors must remain unconscious of audience in Beckett's plays – Alienation *versus* revulsion – Possible dangers of reading or seeing Beckett's plays, as outlined by a psychiatrist (unpublished) – How is a mental state made dramatic? – The artist is not a clinical case   43

3 A BIG PALE BLUR IN THE GREAT DEEPS

Psychodrama, drama as therapy – For whom? – Enactment of problems of self – *Victims of Duty* – Ontological insecurity – Dreams and nightmares – *Endgame* and warfare within the split psyche – Crucial relations between the 'inside' and the 'outside' – Endlessness a source of fear – Reactions to the double-bind situation in *Godot* – Visionary, not personalistic works   58

4 DRAMATIC INTENSITY

It is intensity of response that has to be assessed – Short-term and long-term effects – Progressive limitation and intensification in Beckett's plays contrasted with enlargement of imaginative horizons in Ionesco – *Jeux de Massacre* and *Endgame* as a double bill – Beckett's contrapuntal technique – The theme of transience (Heidegger, George Herbert, Bossuet, Musset, Ionesco, Beckett and the Bible: *Breath* – Irony – Serio-comedy – The quality of silence – Pinter's *Landscape and Silence* – Norwid and silence – Poetic power – Structural and archetypal hermeneutics – Archetypal images in Beckett and Ionesco – The manuscript of *Godot* – Engulfment by time: *Happy Days*, *Victims of Duty*, *Slime* (*La Vase*), *Endgame* – The structure of *Godot* and *Endgame*, and Jungian mandalas: balance and wholeness – Beckett's circular structures and Ionesco's horizontal structures – Assessing dramatic effectiveness – Catharsis – Individual reactions and general truths   71

5 THE SPECTATOR SPEAKS

The critic as spokesman for the spectator – Why and how the Beckett Survey was undertaken – A few striking results – The cosmic equation   98

FINALE

The image of Man   105

NOTES   112

APPENDICES

I *The Beckett Survey:* Questionnaires – Tables   116
II Some Replies to Open-Ended Questions   129
III A Beckett-Ionesco Chronology   144
IV Select Bibliography   146

INDEX OF THEMES AND IDEAS   148

INDEX OF NAMES AND TITLES   152

Introduction

This is primarily a study of the plays of Samuel Beckett, an attempt to explain their effectiveness in the theatre. However, rather than concentrate solely on Beckett's plays I have chosen to consider them alongside the major plays of Eugène Ionesco, in the hope that the comparison will lead to greater illumination. Why Ionesco?

When Eugène Ionesco was asked what he thought of the award of the Nobel Prize for Literature to Samuel Beckett, he was reported as saying, 'Nous l'avons mérité'. The remark, whether apocryphal or not, is a precise indication of the extent to which the names of Beckett and Ionesco have become firmly welded together in the public mind since they achieved prominence in the mid-1950s as the most original exponents of the then avant-garde theatre. Their names are so often bracketed together as the leading exponents of the 'theatre of the absurd' that they are in danger of meeting the same fate as Debussy and Ravel, Addison and Steele, or Rawicz and Landauer. One might object that if there is any real risk of their being thought of as symbiotic twins, it is only among the non-specialist members of the public that this could happen; but critics given to generalising (solely in the public interest, of course) are sometimes equally to blame. Gerald Weales, for example, called them 'France's angels of darkness'*. William Saroyan referred to them as 'the only men of science among the dramatists we have'†. One small book published in the 1960s, whose author and title I have now mercifully forgotten (I do remember it claimed to be of particular use to students and that it was published in France),

* 'Theatre I', *Kenyon Review*, vol. XX, No. 2, spring 1958, p. 303.
† *Ionesco*, pp. 207–8. This makes sense in terms of Baudelaire's idea that 'imagination is the most *scientific* of the faculties'.

dismissed Ionesco, Beckett and Adamov in half a page, because their writings *lack order*, merely lead to pessimism and – horror of horrors – they are *not really French*.

Kenneth Tynan has contributed to the blurring, by referring to 'plays of the Beckett-Ionesco genre' and calling them 'essentially Western, addressed to and written by members of a sophisticated intelligentsia in countries with a high standard of living. The questions they pose', he suggests, 'could be summarised thus: once a man's physical needs are satisfied, what is the purpose of living?'* Oddly enough, this is intended to be an adverse criticism of the two playwrights. In fact it is rather an insult to members of society who do not belong to the well-off sophisticated intelligentsia; they are apparently not supposed to think about the purpose of living. It must be said, however, that Tynan went on to draw a distinction between Ionesco's 'facile and despondent philosophy' (p. 201) and Beckett's 'tragic honesty that Aeschylus would have recognised, if not comprehended' (p. 190).

If one needs another dramatist to act as a foil to Beckett, then, one could not do better than choose Ionesco, bearing in mind the two important features their plays have in common: they are written with the minimum of conscious manipulation and applied technique, and they are created out of a deeply-felt existential anguish—hence, they frequently elicit similar kinds of response from empathic spectators. The similarities soon begin to fade, however, when viewed together in detail. Where Ionesco leaves off, Beckett begins.

The basic concern throughout these pages, then, will be to try and discover and describe and account for the function and effect of the dramatic structures of Beckett (and to a lesser extent of Ionesco) as a form of inner exploration leading to deeper self-knowledge not only for the playwright but particularly for the spectator. If a reciprocal reaction takes place between ourselves and Beckett's plays in performance, we may still have the puzzled frown at the end, but we are conscious of

* *Tynan on Theatre* (Pelican Edition), 1964, p. 188.

the implicit interrogation; we are being asked, 'Where are *you* going from here?'

Public taste and theatrical sophistication have gone through a revolution since the early 1950s, when Beckett and Ionesco began their career as dramatists. The indignation and perplexity of many theatre-goers at that time indicate the extent to which habit-forming conventional well-made realistic plays had blunted receptiveness. The unease that was felt was not unlike that provoked by the first Impressionist paintings or *Le Sacre du Printemps;* well-tried aesthetic attitudes suddenly ceased to be useful guides as to what distinguished 'good art' from a mere hoax. 'Avant-garde', absurdist plays had been written and performed, to small audiences, since the end of the nineteenth century, of course, and yet when *Waiting for Godot* was first put on in the mid-fifties most critics and audiences on both sides of the Atlantic found it upset their common expectations of what a good play should be. *Godot* came on to the scene when the theatre was pretty much a desert, dominated by Rattigan and Anouilh (admirable in their highly-skilled and entertaining professionalism, but backward-looking). This may be one of the reasons why *Godot* created so much impact, scandal and *malaise*. At that time in Western Europe generally there was a strong feeling of post-war disillusion. The age of heroes and of action for good causes had temporarily gone. Perhaps an increasing number of intelligent young people felt the need to ponder about the ultimate questions posed by existence. *Godot* seemed to match the mood of a large enough number of people to keep it alive during the first few vulnerable months of its public life. Here was a play which both entertained and disturbed in a completely new and revolutionary way. How it achieved this will be the subject of many of the following pages.

When I asked Beckett whether he thought there was anything in the situation of theatre at the time *Godot* appeared which helped it on its way, his reply was typically unhelpful: 'I don't know. I never expected it to be produced or to last more than a few weeks when it was put on.' This conversation took place in a pub beside the Royal Court Theatre, where *Godot* was in rehearsal. Anthony Page ('a very talented young man', Beckett commented) was directing it, and Beckett was keeping a watching brief. I had written to him a couple of weeks before, having heard he was coming over, and he agreed without much enthusiasm to meet me and talk about *Waiting for Godot* (of which I had undertaken a critical edition in the hope of getting to understand it myself). On that cold day in January 1965 I went hopefully to Sloane Square, feeling as though I was to be given a half-hour séance with Shakespeare or Racine—anyone who thinks this exaggerated should read George Devine's account in *Beckett at Sixty*:

> To meet Samuel Beckett for the first time must be described as the experience of a lifetime . . . In that half-hour, I was in touch with all the great streams of European thought and literature from Dante onwards. . . .

I waited at the stage door for a couple of minutes. Beckett came out, looking as if he might change his mind. He stood still on the pavement, his hands deep in the pockets of his sheepskin jacket. 'I'm no good at talking about my work, you know. I can't be much help to you.' I made reassuring noises and promised him I was not going to ask him stupid questions such as "Who is Godot". He bought the first pint, we found a table, talked about rehearsals. Gradually he stopped looking as though he would take flight any moment. We began to talk about *Godot*.

c.d.: The papers say you are using a 'new text' of *Godot*. What changes are there?
s.b.: Nothing new—just the Grove Press text, if the Lord Chamberlain will allow it. *I prefer it to the French text anyway.*
c.d.: What do you think of Lionel Abel's view [in *Metatheatre*] that *Godot* can be understood only in terms of your relationships with James Joyce?
s.b.: Nonsense.

c.d.: Is Lucky's speech intended to be a parody of the Joycean style?

s.b.: No.

c.d.: Does Godot come in the interval?

s.b.: No.

(This disposed of some of the theories that I had read about previously.)

c.d.: Do you feel a desire for self-destruction in the face of the horrors of the world?

s.b.: The autobiographical aspect is not in the least important in *Godot*. I express no personal opinions in it.

(This was not quite an answer, but I left it there.)

c.d.: Were the symmetrical beauty and balance of *Godot* achieved without preparation?

s.b.: Yes. I didn't have too much trouble with it.

(Considering that *Waiting for Godot* has an inimitable combination of sheer simplicity of form and complexity of metaphysical implication, I felt this to be an understatement, but as I found out when I studied the manuscript months later, he was telling nothing less than the truth.)

c.d.: Do you care about being understood as *you* wish to be?

s.b.: I'm not interested in the effect my plays have on the audience. I simply produce an object. What people think of it is not my concern.

c.d.: It seems to me that like Giraudoux you adopted a more accessible style for the theatre.

s.b.: Playwriting was a relief from the terrible kind of prose I was writing at that time. I just thought I would try it out.

c.d.: What do you think the theatre is for?

s.b.: I don't know. *I'm not interested in the theatre.* I very rarely go to see other people's plays – only to see friends acting in fact.

(This has be be viewed in the light of the fact that Beckett is very interested in seeing his *own* plays on stage [preferably in the semi-private situation of rehearsal rather than at a public performance]. Ionesco has also said he does not like theatre.)

At this point I got up to have our glasses replenished and to fetch a couple of cheese rolls. When I got back Beckett, to my surprise, was still there. As we munched he talked about Godeau and *Mercadet*, two genetic theories that have by now entered *Godot* lore. 'This was an anecdote I was told', he said, 'about a group of people waiting around after a cycle race in France. "Qu'est-ce qu'on attend?" someone asked. "On attend Godeau." This was the name of a veteran champion cyclist. It was after writing the play I was told about this', he added. He later confirmed this in a letter. The chronology seemed to me of interest, as Hugh Kenner had built up a theory (in his *Samuel Beckett*, p.124) that depended on Beckett's having heard the story before writing the play. Godeau was also the name of the unseen hero of Balzac's play, *Mercadet*. Godeau is anxiously awaited to solve all Mercadet's financial problems. Eric Bentley (in *What is Theatre*) pointed out the analogy in 1956. However, Beckett said: 'I didn't read *Mercadet* until after I had published *Godot*.' This may seem strange for a one-time lecturer in French, but *Mercadet* is hardly essential reading.

C.D.: Is a Christian interpretation of the play justified?
S.B.: Yes, Christianity is a mythology with which I am perfectly familiar. So naturally I use it.

(This does not imply, of course, that it is a Christian play. In fact when one applies the doctrine of the Second Coming to it the result is devoid of all hope, *mais n'anticipons pas*.)

C.D.: What are the important questions you tried to raise in *Godot?*
S.B.: I didn't want to raise any intellectual problems. I don't regard myself as a commentator on social things.

(As my question was aimed really at his philosophical intentions, not at his social preoccupations, which were obviously minimal, I had another shot.)

C.D.: What are the aspects of *Godot* you would try to illuminate if you had to write a study of it?

s.b.: I'd be quite incapable of writing a critical study of my own works.

(The remark emphasises one of the important differences between Ionesco and Beckett. Ionesco has a critical *alter ego* which is always willing to comment on his creative self and its works.)

Finally, Beckett told me that if I happened to be in Paris any time, I could have a couple of hours with the manuscript of *En attendant Godot*. I made a point of going there specially in April (1965), and found Beckett in an affable mood, just back from rehearsals of *Godot* in Berlin. Soon I was left alone with the manuscript. A warm April afternoon, in a room with a beautiful view over Paris, just me, and a notebook, and a priceless manuscript that I could see for two hours and never again. I have no idea what the view was. I did not lift my eyes from that exercise-book of two hundred pages or more. Neither before nor since have I worked with such feverish concentration, trying at first to come to terms with the close, spidery handwriting, then working out rapidly what were the most important revelations it held. I went to the key spots: the entrances and exits of characters, Lucky's speech, the other long speeches, the more closely-textured dialogue, and the more heavily-corrected places. The results of all this have been published in my edition of *En attendant Godot*.

At 4 p.m. Beckett wheeled in a trolley bearing an enormous silver teapot, a gigantic tea-cup, and a large milk jug. In the jug stood a large tube of condensed milk, for which he apologised. 'I don't get any milk delivered up here.' After tea, and whisky (or whiskey), and more talk, I took my leave.

Samuel Beckett has said, then, that he is not interested in the effect his plays have on other people. Yet this is one of the most curious phenomena in present-day theatre. *Godot* was revolutionary not only from the stylistic and technical points of view, but also because it placed actors and spectators in an entirely new relationship with each other. Little attempt has been made till now to find out how spectators react to Beckett's plays. Critics have often said how the plays affect *them*, and often make unwarranted assumptions about how others have responded. In this study an attempt is made – rather tentatively and incompletely – to rectify this situation, by including the results of a survey of audience reaction to performances of *Waiting for Godot* and *Endgame*. The steadily increasing popularity of Beckett's plays with young audiences led me to ask the Young Vic to co-operate with the idea in the first place. When I heard that Peter O'Toole's notable production was going to the Nottingham Playhouse early in 1971 I thought there might be some interesting comparisons to be made in the way the two differing types of audience responded to two very different productions.

Apart from young people, there is one other social group whose lack of ingrained theatrical expectations left them wide open to the impact of a Beckett play: long-term convicts. Martin Esslin has made well known (in *The Theatre of the Absurd*, p.14) the reaction of fourteen hundred convicts in San Quentin penitentiary when they saw *Godot* in 1957. They wrote a series of articles in their prison newspaper showing how the play had expressed their own situation by virtue of the fact that its author expected each spectator to draw his own conclusions. Less well known is the sequel to this remarkable theatrical event. Martin Esslin told it at the Symposium which opened the Beckett Exhibition at Reading in May 1971. The following year some prisoners put on their own production of *Waiting for Godot*, and from that a Drama Society flourished in the prison. It was so successful that in 1970 they had written a play and had been paroled in order to tour the United States with it. A very striking example of the therapeutic value of avant-garde drama. Lest we should smile complacently and think to ourselves that the reactions of long-term convicts have nothing to do with us, we should bear in mind that they were experiencing very acutely, if without sophistication, a sensation Beckett feels and externalises, of imprisonment within the boundless walls of the universe, from which there is no escape. His latest published work to date (though not the last to be written), *Le Dépeupleur*, is a vivid expression of this. Inside a vast cylinder fifty metres round and sixteen high (for harmony's sake) live about two hundred bodies, each awaiting its de-populator, its liberator. The cylinder is 'vast enough to allow the search to be in vain. Limited enough for all flight to be vain' [my translation]. This extraordinary piece of prose, forty-nine pages long, defies categorisation; it is an intensified, inverted expression of the vision of the imprisoned existence described in *The Unnamable*:

> Enormous prison, like a hundred thousand cathedrals, never anything else any more, from this time forth, and in it, somewhere, perhaps riveted, tiny, the prisoner, how can he be found, how false this space is, what falseness instantly, to want to draw that round you, to want to put a being in there, a cell would be plenty . . .

A common factor in all of Beckett's dramas is that the figures portrayed are all imprisoned. Some can move away for a short time, in a restricted area, but they are all quite incapable of extended mobility, which forces our attention upon the extent to which we normally depend on mobility—both in life and in literature. Mobility offers the chance of *escape* from an undesirable situation, and the possibility of *communication* with other beings outside our immediate vicinity. Without mobility we are reduced to a vegetative, passive existence. But we are mobile, are we not? We can globe-trot, we can make the pattern of our life change through the exercise of will, so Beckett's portrayal does not reflect, express, comment upon or illuminate our human condition as we see it. Is that not so? On the other hand, our area of choice is strictly limited by time and space. Man is limited by his achievement, he will never reach infinity. Perhaps to within one step of infinity, but never *there*. Man is imprisoned within his life-span, but for Beckett it is not so simple as it is for those who believe there is an end to it. Most of us cling to the idea of continuation or resurrection of identity, but supposing this means going on *for ever?* Will not the end be increasingly desired as it draws near? Shall we not long to be freed into a state of blessed nothingness? This depends on the quality of the existence in store for us, and about this we are mercifully ignorant, although we may entertain private hopes.

Beckett represents for us, in many varied images and forms, the imprisonment of the human consciousness within the bounds of infinity and eternity—not very promising ground, on the face of it, for fiction and drama. He has faced the challenge of the intransigent nature of the subject by scaling down the dimensions of the problem without changing its fundamental elements. He shows us human destiny in an accelerated, concentrated form, and he manages to remain amusing and compassionate while he is doing it. The vision is dark, but laughter lends wings.

I *The Mortal Coil*

For a considerable time now, mortality has been a fact of life, a problem of philosophy, and a commonplace in literature. What is remarkable is not that the problem of mortality is at the root of serious thought and literature of all ages, but that it is a matter we have to be constantly reminded of and brought face to face with, by writers who have more courage than we have. Consider *Richard II*, for example: according to Ionesco, it is 'an illustration of that truth we don't think about, but which is nevertheless simple and infinitely banal: I die, you die, he dies . . .'. The whole concept of the 'absurd' in modern literature is based on the ludicrous contrast between Man – a finite being – and the infinite universe he is thrust into.

One of the characteristics shared by Beckett and Ionesco is their preoccupation with the shuffling off of this mortal coil, and what lies beyond that bourn whence no traveller returns. The problem Beckett poses is, in Ionesco's words, *la fin dernière de l'homme*, 'the ultimate end of Man'. Ionesco wants theatre to have an impact on the common man, *par-delà son ignorance*, beyond the realm of what he knows or does not know; a theatre based on the fact that the essential condition of man is not as a citizen, but as a mortal. Ionesco has called Beckett's plays supreme examples of what avant-garde theatre should be, as they return to the source of human anguish and avoid the ephemeral problems of any particular society. He considers that Beckett is essentially tragic because he brings into play *la totalité de la condition humaine*. For both of them mortality is the factor that dictates their attitude towards a problematic existence whose reality and validity (in objective terms) seem to be very doubtful. Their writings are desperate attempts to come to terms with the very fact of existence, which they regard not as a beneficent gift from God, but either as a punishment for an unknown crime or, at best, a huge joke, the enormity and maliciousness of which we cannot even begin to understand.

Many people find this disconcerting. For the person with no religious faith, however, it is an authentic view of the human condition, so let us consider the matter in the terms which cause so much anguish in the minds of these two outstanding exponents of contemporary uneasiness of mind. What is left of Man when he has nothing left? When everything has gone—work, everyday trivial problems, family, the hard-won achievements? When the only newspapers are old ones, when plans for the future have become regrets for the past, when there is no particular reason for doing anything any more? How does one evaluate one's existence when it is no longer propped up by activity and purposefulness, when it is a stark existence which won't allow one to hide behind busy-ness in order to come to terms with it? It is no good objecting that one simply does not view one's existence like that, because there must come a time when we cannot fool ourselves any longer, and that is the moment when we realise that death is close upon our heels.

The fact that works of literature or theatre which deal with such problems are almost immediately labelled 'pessimistic' or 'despondent' is the measure of our determination to stick our heads in the sand. However, even the clear-sighted and the far-sighted may well object that these are legitimate preoccupations for the philosopher and the theologian, perhaps even the poet, but what is the dramatist doing in this *galère?* This is what we have to discover, and in order to find out how these age-old speculations about the purpose of existence and the nature of death have been *humanised* by the creative writer, it is important that the discussion be kept relevant to the dramatist's vision and competence. At the back of one's mind one should have this question: 'How are the language and style of conceptual discourse adapted by the dramatist to the emotional and intuitive role his art plays in relation to the spectator?' However much one reads and knows the thoughts of Stoics and Epicureans – Lucretius, or Seneca, Epictetus or Marcus Aurelius, for example – one is usually aware that it is to our reason that an appeal is being made. They claimed that if one convinces oneself of the inevitability of death one can die freed from the obsessive anguish caused by the prospect of death. 'To avoid fear of death,' Seneca wrote to Lucilius, 'never stop thinking about it.' But such exhortations touch our intellect, not our instinct. We understand, but we are not concerned. As Merleau-Ponty said, *savoir n'est pas éprouver*—'to know is not to experience'. Theatre is above all things an experiential form of art—not an intellectual one.

This, then, is the challenge the dramatist faces if he chooses to deal with the most profound and mysterious philosophical and human problem: mortality. How can he do it without boring and sermonising us? How can he render that state of non-being that is death in dramatic terms? Sartre, in *Huis clos*, and Shaw, in *Don Juan in Hell*, really skirt round the problem in the same way as Sutton Vane with his ingenious *Outward Bound*, by making the state of death an extension of the state of life. The characters' existence consists of attempts to resolve the personal and social difficulties they created for themselves before death.

It would, of course, be wrong to think that every time a dramatist kills off a character or two (even in harrowing circumstances) or makes them talk about death, he is dealing with the problem of mortality. Giraudoux, for example, makes Amphitryon and Alcmene discuss death when they are certain it is imminent for them; but they do not talk about mortality, they talk about *separation*, about the sadness of not being able to grow old together. Once they have imagined themselves experiencing life together as a devoted old couple they can say without concern, 'Let death come!' It is a moving testimony to

25

the power of loyal and sincere love, but it gives us no insight into the problem of mortality.

The distinction between the portrayal of death (or play-acting) and the experience of death is the major theme of Tom Stoppard's *Rosenkrantz and Guildenstern are Dead*, in which the influence of Beckett is so manifest that it is doubly relevant here. The Player says in his professional manner, 'In our experience, most things end in death.' Guildenstern turns on him scornfully, snatches a dagger from the Player's belt and holds it menacingly at his throat. 'I'm talking about death', he says quietly as the Player backs away nervously,

> —and you've never experienced *that*. And you cannot *act* it. You die a thousand natural deaths—with none of that intensity which squeezes out life . . . and no blood runs cold anywhere. Because even as you die you know you will come back in a different hat. But no one gets up after *death*. There is no applause. There is only silence and some second-hand clothes, and that's—*death*.

He pushes the dagger into the Player's throat right up to the hilt, and he dies a dramatic and convincing death. Guildenstern comments that it was his destiny to die like that, with no explanations . . . and then the Player stands up again, brushes himself down, takes his fake dagger from the astonished Guildenstern, and gives the other side – the theatrical side – of the story: 'Deaths for all ages and occasions! Deaths by suspension, convulsion, consumption, incision, execution, asphyxiation and malnutrition! Climactic carnage, by poison and by steel! Double deaths by duel . . .'. But Guildenstern insists on distinguishing between the *moment* of death and the *state* of death: 'Death is not anything . . . death is not . . . It's the absence of presence, nothing more . . . the endless time of never coming back . . .'.

The distinction serves to illustrate the fundamental difference of emphasis to be found in the works of Ionesco and Beckett. Ionesco is concerned with (if that is not too lukewarm a term) the validity of selfhood at the moment of death, whereas Beckett lays stress on the endless time. Or again, as Guildenstern neatly puts it, 'Death followed by eternity . . . the worst of both worlds.' For both the Irishman and the Rumanian the fact that the absurdity of life is eventually topped by the humiliation of death is a constant reminder of the fundamental meaningless-ness of our acts, thoughts and achievements. Their writings are the human record of their ceaseless efforts to come to terms with the mortality of man. But they do not use this anguish as a theme for literary treatment; their writing is a by-product of their obsession, a relentless exploration within themselves in search of a sense of integrated personal selfhood, an attempt to com-pensate for the shapelessness of the universe by creating structures of words, thought, and images.

In *The Killer* Ionesco gives his hero, Bérenger, a sense of permanence, indestructibility and immortality that is patheti-cally self-deceptive. 'A song of triumph arose from the depths of my being', he says. 'I *was*, I realised I had always been, that I was no longer going to die.' Then without any effort Death dispenses with Bérenger, whose fine-sounding speeches of revolt are shown to be just words. 'Words fall like stones, like corpses,' wrote Ionesco. Being dead, they cannot communicate anything. All languages are dead languages. The only alternative to dead language is silence, and to this Bérenger is ultimately reduced, in a final scene of tremendous power. With great eloquence he argues his case against Death (the stage direction tells us it is 'an eloquence that should underline the tragically worthless and outdated commonplaces he is advancing'). Logic, reason, morality, justice—he appeals to them all. The Killer answers with a giggle. Finally, unable to fire the pistols he has so bravely flourished in defiance, Bérenger sinks to his knees, pleading, powerless before the horror of his own mortality. Bérenger, Everyman, Man, you and I, go down before the Killer's silent knife, the symbol of the remorseless, irreparable, biological fact of death.

But what of Man's spiritual strivings? Do they have no place in this grim picture? Of course they find expression in Ionesco's picture of the human condition, symbolised by the poetic image of the beautiful city of light, that haven of Man's struggle against the chaos of material existence. The radiant city, *la cité radieuse*, turns out to be as vulnerable as Man himself, and it is destroyed by the presence of the unknown Killer who (like Camus's plague, *le mal*) cannot be eradicated because he is the embodiment of Man's tragic predilection for destruction and evil.

Bérenger is a very ordinary man—just as Vladimir and Estragon are ordinary men, and Winnie, in *Happy Days*, is an ordinary woman. It is through this very ordinariness that their creators succeed in giving us the *feeling* of the absurdity of existence, where the philosopher can give us only the *concept* and the novelist can give us only the description, to which we respond with varying degrees of equanimity. (This is not to decry the power of the novel, but the vicarious experience of novel-reading is of quite a different order from the intensity of theatrical response—a point to which we shall return.)

Those who know only Ionesco's earlier, shorter plays written in the farcical mode (*The Bald Soprano*, *The Future is in Eggs*, or *Jacques*, for instance) may find it hard to realise that it is theme of death that gives his work its unity. The fundamental identity binding humanity together, to which Ionesco claims he tries to cling, is fear of death. 'Most people do not know they are going to die', he told Claude Sarraute, 'I just inform them of it, that's all.'[1] He is surely wrong here: people know it all right, they just choose to forget it, out of self-deception perhaps, or as protection against despondency. How can we live and pursue ambitions, engage in ultimately senseless and frivolous controversies and occupations *unless* we don an armour of social attitudes and platitudes? This is our dilemma: complacency is to be despised, but it is a comfort. Lucidity brings awareness, but with it comes anguish. It has been said that Ionesco has 'a childish fear of death,'[2] but he refutes this: '. . . I am not terrified, no, I am profoundly humiliated by my insignificance. How can One do this to me! . . .'

As attempts at the articulation of anguish Ionesco's plays have a clearly therapeutic value for *him*. 'Fear is born out of repression of the death-instinct', he maintains.[3] It is for this reason that he has determinedly not suppressed this fear, but has exteriorised it in what we may advisedly call his psychodramas, notably *Le Roi se meurt* (*Exit the King*) (1962), *Le Piéton de l'air* (*A Stroll in the Air*) (1962), and *Jeux de Massacre* (1970). Before writing *Exit the King* he had been seriously ill, and had felt the touch of death upon him. He wrote the play *pour me faire la leçon à moi-même*, to prime himself.

King Bérenger is told something by his doctor that he never expected to hear: he is dying. 'But I know that,' he exclaims, 'of course I do! We *all* know it. You can remind me when the time comes. You have a mania for disagreeable conversation early in the morning . . .'. He asks for his breakfast—but finds he is not very hungry. His tongue is coated, he needs some pills. His liver is all choked up, and he has a nasty taste in his mouth. Importunately his doctor returns to the subject: 'You *are* going to die.' With understandable acerbity, King Bérenger retorts, 'What, again! You get on my nerves! I'll die, yes, I'll die all right. In forty, fifty, three hundred years. Or even later. When I want to, when I've got the time, when I make up my mind. Meanwhile, let's get on with affairs of state.' But all the signs of physical deterioration – those very same signs that constantly assail the characters of Beckett's plays as well – gradually convince him of his mortality. He falls to the ground, he loses his powers. Queen Marguerite tells him there is no reprieve; he has lived avoiding the thought of death, like any *common* man. A king should show himself more far-sighted than ordinary mortals. He must now play his part, *as a mortal*. Not as a king, shackled to his duties, not as a workman labouring with his tools, not as a soldier. All the accoutrements of these social roles are removed from him by the queen who attends him. His empire crumbles to dust as the senses with which he perceived it cease to function—he is the sole witness to its reality. His power of speech goes, his heart has no need to beat any more, he does not need to breathe. As he dies, the queen says, 'It was a lot of fuss about nothing, wasn't it?' A deliberately ambiguous remark: life was a fuss about nothing, rebelling against death was too. One by one, every object round the king vanishes, and the moment of his death is marked by his own physical disappearance, leaving an empty throne on an empty stage.

What *leçon* can we deduce from this? Teleportation, trans-substantiation, annihilation? It is not Ionesco's aim to speculate in this play about the self's existence after death, only to show the misery caused by refusal to face up to the inevitability of death, as though one could be exempt through some sort of superiority. Unfortunately Ionesco found that the lessons he wanted to give himself did not help him at all, although he hoped it might help others.[4]

From the visual and dramatic point of view *Exit the King* provides excellent theatre, striking spectacle and distinctly interesting problems for the set designer to solve. Beyond that it is not altogether satisfactory; not that Ionesco should tell us what he thinks happens to King Bérenger—few of us are now so naive as to think that art should give answers. We are content if it makes human problems meaningful to us by appealing to our intuition and imagination. No, *Exit the King* is less than satisfactory because the kind of enlightenment (based on imaginative speculation) that we need should *begin* at the point of Bérenger's disappearance. Preparing ourselves for death is little help when one comes to consider the infinitely more interesting and complex matter of the nature of the Self which either disintegrates or continues in some form or other after death. This is the matter that forms the ground bass of the richly speculative world of Beckett's novels and plays—a realm of experience very much more grim than that of Ionesco, for Beckett has pursued the problems of Time, Being, and Existence much more ruthlessly than Ionesco has. *Exit the King* leaves one with the feeling of being cheated, as one would if *Waiting for Godot* ended with Vladimir and Estragon giving up and going away, or if Clov were to open the door and wheel Hamm out into the open spaces beyond their refuge, or if *Happy Days* finished with Willie picking up a spade and digging Winnie out of the ground.

At the end of *Exit the King, Rhinoceros,* and *The Killer,* Ionesco imbues the situation with an elevation which has all the qualities of true tragedy—and then deliberately mocks and destroys it, thus appearing to question the possibility of a true tragic experience. For all the brave stands he takes against the impending dangers he faces, Bérenger is a mock tragic hero—just as the Smiths and the Martins in *The Bald Soprano* are parodies of comic characters. Ionesco stated that his intention in *The Chairs* (1951) was to pass through farce, to the climax where the sources of the tragic lie. He designated this play a tragic farce, but it would be nearer the mark to call it a farcical morality play.

In Beckett's plays there are no heroic stands, either parodied or genuine. A brief review of their endings will show a common feature:

Waiting for Godot: 'Shall we go?'—'Yes, let's go.' (*They do not move.*)

All that Fall: Jerry says, 'A child fell in to the line, under the wheels of the train.' He runs away. The sound of the wind and the driving rain gradually drown the dragging footsteps of Dan Rooney and Maddy.

Endgame: Clov is standing by the door. Hamm thinks he has abandoned him at last. 'Since that's the way we're playing it,' he says, 'let's play it that way, and speak no more about it.' *He covers his face with his bloody handkerchief, and sits back motionless. Tableau. Curtain.* (One might say Hamm is heroic, or better, stoic; but his self-awareness prevents his making any heroic *stand.*)

Krapp's Last Tape: 'Perhaps my best years are gone. When there was a chance of happiness.' He sits motionless, letting the tape run on in silence.

Act without Words I: The tormented Beckettian Tantalus ignores everything going on about him. He does not move. He looks at his hands.

Happy Days: Winnie sings her love-song; smiles; she and Willie look at each other. Long pause. Curtain.

In all of these the constant end-factor is silent immobility. Meeting silence with silence, as Vigny would say. The only dignified response to what Lucky calls 'divine apathia, divine athambia, divine aphasia'—God's insensitivity to suffering, his imperturbility, and his inability to hear or respond to Man's supplications.

Ionesco attempts to speculate beyond the dimensions of physical existence in *A Stroll in the Air*, in which he expresses Man's desire for spirituality and for escape upwards from the leadenness of mortality by taking to its extreme the illogical, poetic, almost mystical experience of levitation and evanescence which he had introduced into several of his previous plays (*Victims of Duty, Amédée or How to Get Rid of It, The Killer*, and *Rhinoceros*, for example). Bérenger becomes a *piéton de l'air* (as the French title has it), a walker-on-air who takes rather more than the 'stroll' of the English title. After catching sight of a visitor from the anti-world (the origin of everything that exists, yet so small it has no dimension) Bérenger becomes convinced that he has only to break through the void of nothingness to find everything restored and reconstructed on the other side. Full of the desire for permanence beyond mortality, he flies up into the sky. But from the tale he tells on his return it is clear that Ionesco sees no possibility of escape from materiality in an outward direction from the self. All that lies beyond the earth is a desolate and appalling existence, and on the other side of that, nothingness. With this play Ionesco exploited the sensation of dreamlike flying to its logical and theatrical extreme, at the same time destroying it as a theme. For the meaninglessness of the sensation had at last been revealed. The vision of a world of light had been illusory in *The Killer*, from a rationalist point of view; in *A Stroll in the Air* the conclusion is much more grave and despondent. The vision is shown to be unreal, the aspirations without foundation.

Such aspirations have little place in Beckett's work. For one moment we glimpse them in *Happy Days*, when Winnie asks Willie,

'Is gravity what it was, Willie? I fancy not. Yes, the feeling more and more that if I were not held in this way, I would simply float up into the blue. And that perhaps some day the earth will yield and let me go, the pull is so great, yes, crack all around me and let me out. Don't you ever have that feeling, Willie, of being sucked up? Don't you have to cling on sometimes, Willie?' '*Sucked up*?', inquires Willie. 'Yes, love,' she insists, 'up into the blue like gossamer. (*Pause.*) No? You don't? (*Pause*) Ah well, natural laws, natural laws, I suppose it's like everything else, it all depends on the creature you happen to be.'

The natural law Winnie alludes to is that of Newton relating to the force of gravity. She fondly imagines she is being sucked *up*, when she is in fact being sucked *down*. The spectator does not yet know this, of course. The irony of her delusion (which is quite absent from the French version, since *sucée* could be either up or down) will be silently pointed when the curtain goes up on Act 2 and we see her sunk another six inches into the earth. That, however, is only the superficial irony. The deeper irony is revealed when we realise that the allusion Beckett is making (as distinct from Winnie, who does not always know what she says) is to the natural law of the passing of time, by which she is being relentlessly engulfed. She is being decanted from existence (and not even material existence) into non-existence.

Winnie and Willie are in a different category of existence in which it is no longer valid to talk about 'dying'. It is a dream-like world in which engulfment by time is quite remorseless and complete, as Winnie herself realises when she asserts that those parts of her (and, by extension, those parts of her past experience) which are no longer visible (or within recall) *have never existed*. Thus the play may be seen as a rebuttal of Bergsonian *durée;* it owes as much to Vico's cyclical theory of time as to Zeno, whose heaps of millet grain are a recurring image in Beckett's works.

Beckett's plays are acted out in a kind of purgatory of eternal waiting which has many points of similarity with that of Dante. The influence of Dante on Beckett is very well established, of course, and many mystifying allusions in

C

Waiting for Godot suddenly acquire clarity when reviewed in a Dantesque light. However, the undeclared nature of the setting, the purpose of the waiting and the role of Godot is subtly maintained, with the result that the atmosphere of the play is also much nearer home, at the same time, synchronically. If it bears a resemblance at times to the atmosphere of *All that Fall*, is it not because neither of them takes place very far from Rosscullen, with its 'white springy roads, misty rushes and brown bogs', in *John Bull's Other Island*? Shaw makes it a place of torment in the eyes of Keegan, whom one can easily see – without too much strain on credulity – becoming a Lucky, enslaved to Shaw's Pozzo, Broadbent, busy surveying the syndicate's land.[5]

Since *All that Fall* – unlike Beckett's other plays – has a recognisable, specific setting, waterlogged with Irish dampness and stiff with groaning arthritis, it is tempting to regard it in the same light as Shaw's Ireland or Chekhov's Russia. But the superficial similarity between these torpid worlds and purposeless lives enables us to see more clearly the concern that motivates Beckett's imagination. Michael Robinson has expressed it admirably in his sensitive study of Samuel Beckett, *The Long Sonata of the Dead:* '*All that Fall* is moved by the same anger at the intolerable fact of death which was present in the finer pages of *Watt*' (p. 282). The anger and indignation at the transience of life are the same emotions as those which move Ionesco, but it would appear that the act of shuffling off this mortal coil is not the source of anguish and fear for Beckett as it is for Ionesco, especially in his latest play, *Jeux de Massacre*. Beckett is able to make his references to death not only oblique but rather jocular and tongue-in-cheek, as with the lament for the hen that has been run over in *All that Fall*:

> What a death! One minute picking happy at the dung on the road, in the sun, with now and then a dust bath, and then – bang! – all her troubles over. All the laying and the hatching. Just one great squawk and then . . . peace.

On the subject of death, Beckett's writing is saved from

becoming portentous or dismal by the sudden irruption of
the outrageous. Often he achieves this by means of the deformed
cliché, as in the *Texts for Nothing*: 'Nothing like breathing your
last to put new life into you.' Similarly in *Waiting for Godot*:

VLADIMIR: What about a little deep breathing?
ESTRAGON: I'm tired breathing.

A highly literary and despairing, but nevertheless vigorously
obscene gesture in the direction of death is a common feature
of Beckett's novels and plays. The tone was set in his early
novel, *Murphy* (1938), whose hero leaves instructions in his will
for his ashes to be placed in a paper bag and

> brought to the Abbey Theatre, Lr Abbey Street, Dublin, and put
> without pause into what the great and good Lord Chesterfield
> calls the necessary house, where their happiest hours have been
> spent . . . and I desire that the chain be pulled upon them, if
> possible during the performance of a piece, the whole to be
> executed without ceremony or show of grief.

This not merely a grotesque and irreverent show of defiance;
the juxtaposition of final exit and continuing performance is
deliberate. The implication that life is an existential illusion
is made clear by the house of illusion that Murphy chooses for
his self-debasing demise, *via* its notoriously noisy W.C.

It is not only death that inspires distaste and scorn in Beckett,
but the reverse procedure also – birth – since mortality is
simply the logical outcome of natality. On this point, his views
are totally opposed to those of Ionesco. Let us consider first a
short play by John Whiting, *No Why*. It concerns a boy who
has committed an unspecified crime. No one will say openly
what it is. It eventually transpires that it is the crime of having
been born. The same theme is frequent in Beckett, but he does
not leave the matter there. True, he does say in his essay on
Proust that 'the tragic figure represents the expiation of
original sin, of the original and eternal sin of him and all his
"socii malorum", the sin of having been born'. However, in

Waiting for Godot it seems that the thought has undergone a subtle change:

VLADIMIR: Suppose we repented?
ESTRAGON: Repented what? Our being born?

This has been interpreted as meaning that Estragon accepts the guilt of having been born, but it is surely clear that if Beckett had wished to restate Molloy's obscure feeling of guilt, of having been exiled from an ideal timeless existence into the prison of a suffering world, he would have expressed it as a statement and not as a question. The tone of Estragon's question implies that it is a ludicrous suggestion, this idea of repenting being born; guilty of being born, when we had birth thrust on us, existence forced on us, as part of a huge joke? A joke that goes on too long, since there is no certainty it inspires the last divine cackle at the moment of death? Punished we may be; but *guilty*? If there is any blame to be laid, it is to the 'omni-omni' (as he is called in *Mercier et Camier*) who forced us into being.

In *Happy Days*, which is perhaps Beckett's most uncompromising and grim play, *and* the one most full of human warmth, tenderness and pity, we see him dealing with this question in a fashion which illustrates his consummate art of metaphysical comedy (and let us bear in mind that Ionesco has said, 'the comic is the intuition of the absurd . . . to become conscious of what is horrifying, and to laugh at it is to become master of that which is horrifying'). Winnie's eye is suddenly caught by something crawling along the ground in front of her:

WINNIE: Oh I say, what have we here? Looks like life of some kind! An ant! Willie, an ant, a live ant! Where's it gone? Ah! Has like a little white ball in its arms. It's gone in. Like a little white ball.
WILLIE: Eggs.
WINNIE: What?
WILLIE: Eggs . . . Formication.
WINNIE: What?
WILLIE: Formication.
WINNIE: (*murmur*): God.

Then they both begin to laugh, and this develops into a crescendo and diminuendo of mirth. She goes on:

> Ah well what a joy in any case to hear you laugh again, Willie, I was convinced I never would, you never would. I suppose some people might think us a trifle irreverent, but I doubt it. How can one better magnify the Almighty than by sniggering with him at his little jokes, particularly the poorer ones. . . . Or were we perhaps diverted by two quite different things?

Any form of life is a great surprise to Winnie, as it is to Clov and Hamm in *Endgame*. The way she reacts to the revelation of what the little white ball is can be interpreted in more ways than one (like Estragon's repeated *Ah!* each time he is reminded they are waiting for Godot). The text instructs the actress to 'murmur' the word *God*, but that murmur can express horror or mere surprise. Madeleine Renaud, who should know, puts on a coy, old-fashioned look, bites her lip as if to repress a smile, and murmurs 'Dieu' as though it means 'Really! You are naughty!' This is a delightfully comic moment which leads on naturally to the ensuing laughter, but by saying the word and reacting that way, she changes the meaning of the laughter from its original intention in the English version (which Beckett wrote first). An Englishwoman does not use the word 'God' to mean 'Really! You are naughty!' Winnie, before murmuring the word, is told to pause, lay down her spectacles, and gaze before her (in both the English and French versions). All of this seems to add up to a reaction of *shocked* surprise. She is, surely, appalled. When Willie begins to laugh he breaks her mood, and she joins in, but as she perceptively suggests, they are laughing at quite different things. Willie, with his dirty mind (he has just been looking at a dirty postcard) is laughing at the confusion he has created in Winnie's mind between *formication* and *fornition*, but she suddenly sees how laughable is the ludicrous process of procreation, how ridiculous the dogged determination to perpetuate life in this absurd existence by bringing into existence other creatures who will have to suffer. This is an example of how even a brilliant and authoritative performance can betray a text.

In *Endgame* it is the surprise appearance of a flea in Clov's trousers that inspires in Hamm the fear that 'humanity might start from there all over again', and frenzied application of insect powder eliminates that possibility—they hope. Hamm's fear is consistent with his anger at his own 'accursed progenitor', Nagg, for engendering him. Beckett's attitude towards loving relationships between man and woman is deeply affected by the probability that these relationships will result in another birth, that is, another estrangement from the ideal state of timelessness in which we were before birth. Love, therefore, is a revolting thing, for Beckett's vice-existers.

Ionesco's attitude towards birth is the complete opposite of Beckett's. 'The wish to create beings, that is what divine love is' he writes in his *Journal en miettes* (*Fragments of a Journal*) (p. 109). Only 'creative love, love that gives birth' can be justified. Perhaps the proliferation of objects and people in Ionesco's plays, in contrast to the dematerialised, depopulated world of Beckett, is one of the results of their differing attitudes to creation. The passionate indignation with which Beckett reacts to the process of birth is matched only by that which Ionesco lavishes upon the process of dying.

What is surprising is that Ionesco should have failed to represent, in his most ambitious and comprehensive dramatic expression of his obsession with death, *Jeux de Massacre*, any other reaction than repulsion and melancholy. One would think, merely from this and his other 'mortality plays', that he was unaware that death can be and frequently is faced with calmness and serenity; but his *Journal* shows the contrary. He is fully conversant with the less anguished attitudes—Judaism, Christianity, Buddhism. But his reading of Martin Buber has taught him that although 'the determined exploration of the heart is the beginning of the Way in the life of Man' (p. 95) this exploration can be sterile and lead only to greater self-torture and despair, even if it really leads to the Way.

This realisation has led Ionesco to doubt the efficacy of the self-analysis of private diaries. His own journal shows him to have considerable self-knowledge: 'I know that my malaise comes from the fact that I am separated from myself' (p. 96). Anyone who has read a little Jungian psychoanalytical theory, he says, will realise he suffers from inconsolable separation from his mother, from the *anima*, from the earth, from death—but this does not help at all. There is still an immense wall that stops him *feeling* – not just understanding in the abstract – that 'death is *me*', that 'the depths of self' are 'non-self'. This is the anguished existential fear of non-being that he externalised above all in *Victims of Duty*.

When, asks Ionesco, shall we learn to hope for death instead of fearing it? All humanity should be re-educated to think like the ancient Mexicans, for whom death was the occasion for rejoicing. Of these reassuring attitudes, then, he is fully aware. Yet he has not sought to represent them in his drama. One cannot criticise him for this, for the dramatist is totally free to give whatever vision of existence he wishes, and his alone— Ionesco has had to insist on his right to artistic freedom in just the same way as Chekov had to parry the attacks of Mikhailovsky and Skabichevsky. In *Jeux de Massacre* only one thing transcends death: love. Only in the two scenes showing young love – and old love – and the determination not to be separated by death, does Ionesco show the human race capable of a dignity superior to its mortal condition.

Ionesco fully realises that fear of death comes from being too attached to life, and that if we could demystify Eros, all desires would cease, including the desire to exist (*Journal*, p. 84). This is perhaps what Ionesco had in mind when he called Beckett *le véritable démystificateur*, 'the true demystifier'[6]. The longing for release from consciousness is given dramatic expression with as much insistence and intensity by Beckett as Ionesco gives to his dramatisation of the fear of extinction. However, not only would it be a gross oversimplification to say that whereas Ionesco dramatises his fear of death, Beckett dramatises his desire for annihilation; it would also be a failure to appreciate that the tension in Beckett's plays is frequently derived from the coexistence of the blind but vigorous will to live and the yearning for release from consciousness. The traditional dichotomies of comedy and tragedy, optimism and pessimism, are therefore unhelpful. Nevertheless, one is often reminded, in reading Beckett, of that part of *Revelation* describing the first of the troubles to come: 'When this happens, man will long for death and not find it anywhere; they will want to die and death will evade them' (9. vi).

In *Jeux de Massacre* Ionesco makes the point over and over again that death is an obscenity and a cruel alienation. This play leads on naturally from *Exit the King*, in which one of the consoling thoughts is, 'May everything die with me'. He allows himself the same consolation in *Jeux de Massacre;* it was foreseeable that he would try to escape from the anguished feeling of loneliness in the face of death by involving others. The basic delusion underlying this play is that by dispersing individual anguish into general panic it can be diluted and attentuated. Ionesco therefore treats natural death as an epidemic striking fast and indiscriminately. The spectator quickly realises that each scene will end with the death of those characters who appear most vital or invulnerable. Hence the massacre soon ceases to effect us, because the humans are reduced, Ubu-like, to puppets, even in the more moving scenes. To this there is one exception, the beautiful scene between the Winnie-like old woman and her weary-Willie husband, who realises only when his wife is stricken with the plague that happiness had been around him to enjoy all the time, just as she had always tried to tell him. Apart from this scene, one looks in vain for moments when the dialogue rises above the banality of the repeated theme—moments when the impact will be heightened by the density of the texture, the synchronic suggestiveness of images; in short, the text fails to imply beyond its statement. The oversimplification of ideological and theological arguments is a grave weakness: parodic clichés, for example – 'Poverty is a vice', explains a bourgeois – and caricatural doctors ('People die through ignorance . . . If everyone followed medical precepts conscientiously, no one would die'). The only spiritual resonance in the play is contained in a short scene of comic confessions and in the old man's despairing cry, 'Who can help us, except God! He isn't there'. Ionesco claimed that *Jeux de Massacre* is 'a statement of fact, an objective document'. He went on: 'I'm not taking up any position. I say what there is to be said.'[7] In fact, Ionesco's display of reactions to death is highly personal and selective. The reaction of François-Régis Bastide to the play was to admit it was 'masterful and often heart-breaking', but, he goes on; 'When you come out of a Ionesco play you're even more stupid than when you went in. . . . We are all idiotic. Nothing serves any purpose. The world is done for, finished. Emptiness expressing emptiness.'[8] One is forced to the conclusion that Ionesco took a vast subject he was unable to cope with intellectually and dramatically. Or are we at fault? In his *Journal* Ionesco refers to the desirability of making the audience cease to be aware of itself (p. 147). Perhaps, he suggests, those who thought *Exit the King* banal were unable to get away from the fact of being in a theatre, '. . . and refused to live an adventure which, in a sense, cannot be anything else but banal, of course . . . but which is fundamental if one makes an attempt at living it'. It would be interesting to know if many spectators experienced this sort of empathic participation at a performance of *Exit the King* or *Jeux de Massacre*. Ionesco is absolutely right to stress the importance of empathic transmission of anguish, but his dependence on destructive parody and inconsequential fantasy frequently works against complete audience involvement.

The plays we have been considering attempt to give death the kind of immediacy necessary to make it real to *us* (despite the fact that death is like a hangover: you can have no conception of what it is like until you have experienced it). The more subtle and oblique they are in portraying it, the deeper and more long-lasting is their effect. However, an important question still remains to be answered: why bother to go to the theatre in order to have anguish about death communicated to one? The answer will possibly be clearer when the problems of dramatic exploration of self and dramatic intensity have been dealt with, but one can say at this stage that some of these plays, certainly *Waiting for Godot*, *The Killer*, and *Happy Days*, force the empathic spectator into one of two positions:

Either we enter the realm beyond hope where, stripped of all illusions, we can achieve the serenity and authenticity which Heidegger called *Freiheit-zum-Tode*, freedom in the face of death; *or* we have to admit, if intellectual honesty is our forte, that the plays bring us face to face with what Pascal termed the wretchedness of Man without God.

2 *Exploration and Response*

Samuel Beckett once described his writings as 'my little exploration' – an exploration into that 'whole zone of being that has always been set aside by artists as something unusable – as something by definition incompatible with art'.[9] Kenneth Tynan took Beckett and Ionesco to task for concentrating on 'exploring individual *malaise*', for being anarchic and pessimistic, uninterested in social change, and for rejecting all political solutions. This incensed Ionesco, but Beckett the unrousable would concede, no doubt, that Tynan (or whoever) is welcome to his views. In 1956 Beckett said, 'At the end of my work, there is nothing but dust'. Not very promising material, one might think; and yet Beckett is proclaimed as the most compassionate, remorseless, intellectually honest and difficult writer of our generation. It would be unwise to ignore the fact that this is a remarkable phenomenon, and to take it for granted that dramatisations of private fantasies will be effective. Arrabal is a good example of what happens when the genetic source of plays lies in hatreds and fears (however justified they may be). When drama is used as a means of sado-masochistic revenge, of wildly hitting back, one leaves the theatre after a performance feeling that it must have done the author some good to relieve his emotions, but one's own vision is unchanged. Admittedly, Arrabal is never inept, and if he always reached the level of visionary beauty of *The Car Cemetery*, *The Labyrinth* or *The Garden of Delight* he would show evidence of indisputable artistic discrimination. With *The Architect and the Emperor of Assyria*, technical brilliance cannot compensate for failure to transform the personal nightmare into dramatic vision.

Grotesque cruelty is a form of therapy only for a small proportion of those spectators whose empathic nature enables them to participate fully in the two-way action of theatrical performance. As Arrabal's self-acknowledged master is Beckett, and as Ionesco has written in praise of Arrabal's dramatic vision of the world in terms that really seem to apply to his own plays,[10] Arrabal is relevant to a study of the psychodynamic process that takes place between the playwright and the empathic spectator through the medium of plays created as an essential part of an anguished exploration of self. But with Arrabal one is much more likely to react with the exclamation with which Isadora Duncan greeted Andreyev's *Life of Man*: 'Mon Dieu, c'est une maladie!' The same is true of the early plays of Adamov, who dramatised his nightmares, but nevertheless ended by committing suicide.

Although Jung has warned us that 'a work of art is not a disease', many Anglo-Saxon psychocritics degrade the subject of their analysis by trying to explain the author's neuroses through the confessions called his works. Literary creation thus becomes not so much a noble and privileged activity as a clinical affair composed of infantile phases—oral, urethral, phallic and oedipal.[11] The explication of texts as structures of the mind can be very illuminating, as has been shown by Starobinsky, Rousset (the new Geneva school) and Blanchot,[12] but one looks in vain for a detailed explanation of the effect upon the spectator of theatrical performance, an experience which can set up a more complex series of psychological relationships, and a greater degree of concentrated participation, than any other art-form.[13] Backward-looking criticism, therefore, criticism which seeks the author incarnate in his works, concentrates primarily on the dialogue between the author and his creation. Clearly, this approach is necessary for an understanding of Beckett and Ionesco, but it should be merely a preliminary step towards an understanding of the responses that take place in the re-creative mind of the spectator. Of course, the very dynamism and variability of the relationship between play and spectator make it even more difficult to capture and assess than the static connexion between the act of composition and the written text. It is a virtually inexhaustible investigation.

In order to study the function of the plays of Beckett and Ionesco as a form of inner exploration, we must start from the premiss that literature – and particularly theatre – constitutes an experience through which not only the writer but also the empathic percipient move towards self-knowledge. This 'reciprocal interrogation', as Michel Mathieu calls it,[14] seems worthy of investigation, especially in relation to avant-garde (i.e. non-boulevard) theatre whose function, according to Bernard Dort, is therapeutic.[15] It might be assumed from this that M. Dort has observed the close relationship that is built up between the stage and the auditorium during performances of such plays; how otherwise could a therapeutic action take place? But no, M. Dort stresses the absence of rapport between audiences and this type of '" zero degree" of theatre . . . of which *Waiting for Godot* constitutes the most perfect approximation' (ibid.). It is a spectacle to be looked at, it is a *chose vue*, from which the spectator is detached. Somehow, we have to try and reconcile this assertion of the absence of participation or involvement and the experience of other critics for whom Beckett's plays have a deep subconscious effect that is not merely therapeutic but spiritual or cathartic.

There are those who would challenge the validity or value of examining the nature of theatrical response on the grounds that a play is a play, the text is the thing, an entity in its own right, fully created either on the page or stage without reference to those who observe it. Theodore Shank is among those who reject the idea of the audience being part of the creative process: 'While acknowledging the influence which an audience may have upon a performance,' he writes, 'the way in which I have defined artistic collaborators – that is, as those who make creative choices – eliminates the audience from being so designated' (p. 195). Bernard Dort's opinion is categorically opposed to this: 'the dramatic work has value only in relation to a public. It is created by contact with the public, it changes, is modified, enriched or diminished according to whether the public gives or witholds its approval' (p. 315). Unlike a film, a play is not definitive and complete until it comes face to face with its audiences.

What, one must ask, is the aesthetic status of a play that is being performed without an audience? Is it possible for a work of art to be creative if it is not being experienced? Clearly this is a philosophical question on which opinions will be divided, since it is part of the much larger problem of the objective validity of any action which is not being witnessed or observed. However, we are not concerned with the problem of whether or not an unwitnessed performance is *real*, but of whether or not it has any artistic value. One may say that at play-readings or rehearsals there is no audience, but actors' performances can be of great artistic superiority on such occasions. True; but they are great only because the other actors or readers change roles —they step out of the action and become spectators who alone give the performance a value. May we not agree, then, that as with existence itself, a play acquires a quality of createdness only when it becomes an object of perception?[16]

The three stages that separate an author's initial exploration and subconscious structuring of his fantasies, and the transformation of that experience into subjective meaning by the recipient, are obvious; writer's mind, the text, the reader. In the case of drama there is a fourth stage interpolated: the interpreters (directors and actors). This might indicate that the dramatic work is more remote from the spectator than the novel is from the reader, but this view not only ignores the fact that the play is the play in performance (in print it is just a score), it also ignores the particular quality of dramatic performance, to which Robbe-Grillet draws attention in his essay on 'Samuel Beckett, or "Presence" in the Theatre'.[17] He reminds us that Heidegger said, 'The condition of man is to be *there*.' The theatre probably reproduces this situation, claims Robbe-Grillet, more 'naturally' than any of the other means man has devised to represent reality, for 'the essential thing about a character in a play is that he is "on the scene": *there*' (p. 108). How does a dramatic character differ from a fictional one? By not deceiving us, by appearing, by *being there*—and in all Beckett's major plays, he points out, *being there* means being in the only place that is left. The only presence is the stage presence: 'Everything that is, is here; off the stage there is nothing, non-being.'

Robbe-Grillet's comments ring true for Beckett, but not for Ionesco. One of the most striking and consistent contrasts between their plays lies here: whereas Beckett's non-specific settings enable him to isolate his characters from any social reality that might deflect attention from the generalised human situation he is portraying, Ionesco's domestic settings – an office, a sitting-room, a motor showroom, a busy street, a classroom – are initially ultra-normal. He then reduces these norms to nothing by means of parody, disintegration of language, shock tactics, and farcical *reductio ad absurdum*. He thus tears his characters out of their social condition by their very roots, whilst Beckett's are detached from theirs at the start. Now, when a stage represents a recognisable place, it is *there*, and I am *here*, in the audience, conscious of the fact that I am *not* in an office, street, or classroom. There is a well-defined psychic barrier between me and the inhabitants of that illusory but clearly delineated world, even though I may be totally involved in and fascinated by what they are saying and doing. One would no doubt be held in the same state of attentiveness if one were witnessing a scene between two lovers though a one-way mirror. The spectator is a voyeur. He is always conscious that he is not part of that other well-defined world through the glass wall.

On the other hand, one cannot say with as much conviction that *Waiting for Godot*, *Happy Days*, or the *Acts without Words* are taking place *there* as distinct from *here*, because the locus is quite indefinable. *Endgame* takes place in a domestic setting of a sort, but it is hardly Peyton Place or Coronation Street; a good production in a small theatre draws the circle of isolation, the deserted wastes, round all those who are witnessing this unreal and unusual struggle for survival and mastery. These plays take place nowhere; their cyclic structure indicates their endlessness. They can go on without us. There should be no curtain-calls. We should slink away, not quite certain if it is the end or if we had any right to be there. We have been drawn into an experience—not by the tricks of environmental theatre or the mind-battering assaults of the Living Theatre, but by a delicate and compassionate process that gives Beckett's plays their peculiar haunting quality. 'Haunting' is an imprecise term to use, of course; it is meant to express the effect these plays have (superbly performed) upon the empathic spectator—a sort of gravitational pull that will not let us go emanating from the core of each play. A platonist might say that *Godot* implies an ideal work whose core is not waiting, but absence. *Endgame* implies an ideal work centred on the impossibility of separation and escape. *Happy Days* implies an ideal work whose focus is unremitting extinction that comes too slowly. Many other themes revolve around these axes, but the *absence*, the *imprisonment*, and the *extinction* are the sources of disturbances that can effect the spectator through the cumulative effect of allusions and images.

By the act of creating his plays Beckett organises his own sense of identity; hence, the relationships between his characters are the most important thing about those characters, who are forced into mutual dependence. They depend on each other as guarantors of their existence—even the indomitable Winnie fears that Willie might leave her talking into a void. The Pirandellian overtones of this play-and-life, illusion-and-reality dichtomy will be obvious (*Waiting for Godot* could be subtitled *Tonight we Improvise*). The implications and the intensity of the problem are greater in Beckett than in Pirandello; not necessarily more interesting, but more anguished and concentrated. There is a recipocity of reaction between ourselves (or rather, the empathic percipient) and Beckett's plays (the play affects the spectator's world-view, the spectator completes the significance of the play). This reciprocity sets these plays apart from those of any Pirandellian playwright (Anouilh, for example, or even Ionesco). Why is this?

The relationship between the creatures of illusion on stage in Beckett's plays and the spectator is a confused one. This contrasts with the simplicity of the relationships between the various pseudo-couples (master-slave, parent-child, old friends, husband-wife) which do not undergo great development or change. Their characters are not strongly individualised from play to play (Hamm overlaps with Pozzo, Clov with Lucky, Didi and Gogo are a nascent Hamm-Clov couple). The fragmented psychological cohesion of the characters, together with the absence of a well-defined setting and time-flow during the action, are additional factors which all contribute to the strange pervasiveness of the plays. This lack of specificity is under-scored by frequent allusions to the fact that something is going on which no one understands. The emotional associations created between the ontologically insecure characters, or figures, and the spectator create the illusion of an experience shared. When the spectator's introjective function is fulfilled, the creative process is completed. When Jaspers called this completion the 'beating of the other wing' that gets the work of art off the ground, his image expressed admirably the intimacy between the work and the recipient.

In Ionesco's *The Chairs* the imaginary, invisible audience really exists – within the dimensions of the stage illusion – to the same extent that we, the 'real' audience, do not exist. In Beckett's plays, the characters perform the function of being each other's audience, and it is only for each other that they go on playing their parts, since 'off the stage, there is nothing, non-being'. This includes the auditorium, and any director who makes the actors play out to the audience has not begun to understand that *we do not exist* to Estragon, or Hamm, or Winnie, any more than the imaginary audience in *The Chairs* exists to us. One may rightly object that it is a convention of the theatre that the dramatic action constitutes a temporary form of existence running parallel to that of the audience. Such is the flexibility of our attitude towards the stage action that we unquestioningly permit ourselves to be active participants on a temporary basis (in order to revive Tinkerbell, for example, by our applause). The ambiguous theatricality of *Peter Pan*, of pantomimes, of Anouilh, of the circus, has led some critics[18] to the idea that *Endgame* is aware of itself as a text performed in a theatre, basing themselves on the theatrical terms used in this play, by means of which this effect is achieved—*farce, audition, aside, soliloquy, dialogue, underplot, exit, this is slow work,* and so on. If one wants to be pedantic – and why not if it leads to precision in a situation that is confused enough as it is? – one can object that it is impossible for the *play* to be aware of itself. The *characters* may be conscious of their play-acting role – in common with many characters in Pirandello and Anouilh – but the *play* really cannot be aware of itself. However, having cleared away that minor objection, one can go on to the substantial point, which is that in *Godot, Endgame and Happy Days* the characters are often aware of the need to have an audience. Their audience is not us, however; it is their fellow creatures of illusion. Pozzo demands complete attention to his performance from Estragon and Vladimir, and is very anxious to know what they thought about it afterwards. Hamm wants Clov to listen to his story, and has to bribe Nagg with a bon-bon to be an audience. Nagg's story about the trousers is a failure because he gets no audience reaction. Winnie needs Willie to be the audience for her monologue. All this is important for them because there is no other audience they are aware of. The theatricality of the plays in no way presupposes the existence of an audience outside the action. Hence Beckett's choice of Roger Blin as the first director of *En attendant Godot*: Blin's production of Strindberg's *Ghost Sonata* was at that time, 1950, running to near-empty houses in Paris. Beckett felt that a producer who was able to put on a play so meticulously for no audience was ideal for *Godot*.[19]

These details would seem to reduce severely the importance of the spectator in the creative process, but the contradiction with what has been said previously about the role of the empathic percipient is only apparent. If the two view-points from which we are considering the plays are kept quite distinctly apart, it will be seen that when we consider them as the authentic experiences of autonomous beings existing in a dimension quite isolated from our own, it is essential that the production should make it clear that those beings exist in a void. On the other hand, when the plays are being viewed as dramatic works of art, their full aesthetic potential can be realised and appreciated only through the responses of an empathic observer—just one is quite enough in order to complete the creative process, although that would be rather less than enough for the box-office.

If the actors in Beckett's plays show in any way that they are conscious of the audience's presence, therefore, they automatically falsify the existential situation of the characters they are portraying, since their anguish is caused by the absence of any witness guaranteeing their existence. We complete the (creative) act for the writer, but God would complete the (existential) act for Didi and Gogo ('Do you think God sees me?'), for Winnie ('in and out of someone's eye'), for Hamm ('the bastard doesn't exist'). When the characters refer to role-playing, they are prompted by their *self*-awareness, not by awareness of the audience. There is a good example of what can happen when actors treat Beckett as though he were Oscar Wilde: the first night of the Young Vic's 1970 production of *Endgame* (directed by Peter James) was almost catastrophic. The previews for club members had been justifiably successful, and had given the actors a confident sense of rhythm and timing. At the first public performance, however, there was no response at all. The cast were quite unprepared for playing in a void. They were thrown. The reason was simple, and forseeable: this was the first time the Young Vic's studio, which seats 113, had been used for a major production. Practically fifty per cent of the audience on that first night consisted of critics from the international press. The effect of their professional critical silence was devastating, because the actors had made the mistake of depending on the audience's presence, instead of regarding it as non-existent or, at best, as an intrusion.

The important thing about a Beckett audience is not how they react during performance, but what they feel after it. Sympathetic performance of a Beckett play is thus crucial—Beckett's own increasing interest in production, and his inclusion of more and more stage instructions in his texts (which is not always appreciated by directors and actors who feel their freedom of interpretation being encroached upon), all this is evidence that Beckett is aware of the need to keep as firm a hold as possible on the total creative act. He would seem to be more concerned in recent years with his plays' dramatic (as distinct from literary) impact; it is unlikely that he would say now what he told me in 1964 (in answer to my question about whether he cared about being understood as *he* wished to be): 'I'm not interested in the effect my plays have on the audience', he said. 'I simply produce an object. What people think of it is not my concern.'

The dramatic effectiveness of his plays results from his poetic sense of economy (not Ionesco's strong point), harmony and structure, rhythm and cadence, composed as much of silence as of words. If this delicate balance is botched, there is nothing else to rivet one's attention on. Whereas for well-made plays with strong plots, copious action, recognisable social beings as characters, and well devised suspense to keep one in the auditorium past the ice-cream and coffee break, mere competence is bearable. But not with Beckett. Hence a production of *Waiting for Godot* which cuts across the grain of the text is excruciating to anyone who knows the extreme tension that can be built up by this play. One such example was the American television showing of Alan Schneider's excellent production with Bert Lahr; it was divided into five acts to allow time for the commercials. Another is Adrian Brine's production at the Young Vic (1970), with its pop-music interval and ad-lib circus music. Young people can manage Beckett without these cheap sops. Indeed, the great popularity of Beckett's plays with young people is a phenomenon that deserves some comment. One young man, not a Beckett *aficionado*, explained it to me by saying that young people are ignorant. If we rephrase that in a less biased way, and say that their receptiveness has not yet been blunted by custom and convention, we may be near the mark. The understanding and open-mindedness of the experienced theatre-goer are often constricted by sudden confrontation with revolutionary techniques. *Hernani* in 1830, Wagnerian opera, *Ubu roi* in 1896, *Victor ou les enfants au pouvoir* in 1928, are obvious examples of drama that produced the unease, bewilderment and indignation that is felt when aesthetic attitudes that have served the theatre-goer well suddenly cease to be relevant or useful guides to what is 'good' art and what is mere charlatanry.[20] In the 1950s people with clear ideas of what a good play should be found their expectations upset. They were alienated. But those who were then in their early twenties are now approaching middle age, and they are naturally carrying different norms, more flexible norms, into the auditorium (although it is not certain that this flexibility enables them to appreciate more easily the non-literary frenetic drama of the 1970s). Two generations are now able to look at Beckett, Adamov, Ionesco, Tardieu, and so on, with equanimity and empathy. Is it then still true to say, as Martin Esslin did in 1961, that the Theatre of the Absurd achieves the 'alienation effect' postulated by Brecht very much better than Brecht ever managed to in practice, because 'with such characters it is almost impossible to identify'?[21] The surveys I have carried out of audience reaction indicate that such a view is no longer justified with regard to *Waiting for Godot* or, possibly, to *Endgame*. Audiences no longer have difficulty in identifying with Estragon, Vladimir, Clov (rather than Hamm); Madeleine Renaud has brought so much human warmth to the part of Winnie that her grotesque situation is forgotten. To identify with Bérenger, and even Choubert in *Victims of Duty*, is no longer difficult. Genet's psychopaths, by way of contrast, still alienate with ease, as do the necrophiles and child-murderers of Arrabal. Perhaps by 1980 the present generation of teenagers who revel in Beckett and Ionesco will be able to identify with *The Maids* and with Fidio and Lilbé (the child-killers in *Oraison*), but the great difference is that whereas the characters of Ionesco, Beckett and Tardieu may have alienated because of their strangeness and lack of psychological cohesion, they never caused *revulsion*. Nevertheless, both Beckett and Ionesco have inspired extreme distaste. Wolfe Kaufman said of *Jeux de Massacre*, 'it is a vile, corrupt, depressing, two-hour-long parade of death in each and every possible fashion, striking here, striking there, leaving no escape' (but he had to admit that it was 'vital and vibrant theatre').[22]

Much more violent than this was a letter I received from a doctor, who voiced such a strong protest about the possible dangerous effects of Beckett's plays, that his warning should be quoted at length:

> My daughter has to study *En attendant Godot* at her university and it profoundly disturbs me that this sort of thing should be read by girls of 19. She referred me to your very interesting introduction to the play[23] which reveals an apparent schizophrenic though disorder in *Godot*—strikingly confirmed when one comes to read the text.
>
> There is an excellent and clear account of Schizophrenia in a little text book of Psychiatric Medicine by Curran and Gutmann and the following features are listed by Dr Curran:
>
> (1) Nihilistic ideas
> (2) De-personalisation = loss of sense of 'self'
> (3) De-realisation = loss of sense of reality
> (4) Thought-block
> (5) Failure of communication

(6) Catatonia = spells of physical immobility, as at end of Acts
 I and II
(7) Obscene outbursts
(8) Preoccupation with disorders of excretory functions
(9) Suggestibility
(10) Frenzied outbursts
(11) Periods of silence and inertia
(12) Neglect of personal hygiene
(13) Flight of ideas (e.g. Lucky's speech)
(14) Word 'salds', neologisms, auto-echolalia (Lucky's speech)
(15) Polyvalent ambiguous symbolism, vague metaphysical ideas
 and religious references.

Godot is full of these things. It is interesting to note that Dr
Curran mentions that some schizophrenics are successful in the
theatre, the audience relishing the allusive odd style of talking.

This last point is indeed interesting. *Why* should presumably
'normal' theatre-goers relish plays that are structures of
schizophrenic fantasies? Herein lies a very significant clue
to the relationship between play and spectator that merits
investigation (as we shall see). The letter goes on:

> I do not imply that Beckett himself suffers from the rather
> terrible disorder of Schizophrenia, in spite of the unfortunate
> photograph published with the play, but that he has learned to
> copy its mode of expression. There is certainly a grotesque sense
> of the comic in *Godot* but one would need the sort of literary
> equivalent of coprophilia to find anything 'beautiful' or 'artistic'
> in it if these terms any longer have meaning.
> From a medical point of view it is my opinion that this sort of
> play (and I am sure that *Godot* is far from being the worst of its
> genre) is dangerous to the immature unstable youngsters that
> today seem to gain entrance to our 'universities' if it propagates
> an offensive noxious nihilistic anti-religious idea of life. Adherents
> of this barren idea solace themselves with drugs, sex and uncouth
> behaviour, and arrive at my Hospital Emergency Department
> poisoned or injured. They arrogantly replace the splendid
> positive attitudes which produced the great art of Florence and
> Venice with a series of boring platitudes – *Happy Days* is full of
> them – and wonder why they become miserable. The Chinese
> call it 'seeking the Sacred Emperor in the low-class tea rooms'.
> Somebody ought to make a study of the psychopathology of

novels and plays written since 1918: they are a mine of morbid introspection, nihilism, depression, schizophrenic ideas etc. Freudian free-association and the use of eccentric imagery and vague symbolism is commonplace to any doctor who has attended a psychiatric clinic, but I can understand its apparent novelty to lay persons. It offers an enormous and fascinating field of writing to those without much talent, being very easy to acquire, dispensing with rules and therefore difficulties, and being fashionable. One could write forever, for example, about Willie in *Happy Days* who closely resembles a hebephrenic withdrawn schizophrenic, simply because of his very vagueness and symbolic nature, but there is nothing clever about Beckett in this—I could do the same myself.

As literary criticism the letter has its limitations, but as it is inspired not by virulent ignorance but by genuine concern about the possible effects of a certain type of literature and theatre on unstable readers and spectators, it must give pause for thought. My first reaction was to see the shades of Paul Bourget and François Mauriac rising up with accusing finger.[24] Two things made me feel less guilty: the first was that the doctor's letter was very reminiscent of Jung's original reactions to James Joyce's *Ulysses*—it took him some time to realise its true value in the 'restratification of modern man'. Even the layman, said Jung, would have no difficulty in tracing the analogies between *Ulysses* and the schizophrenic mentality. And yet, he assures us, 'it would never occur to me to class *Ulysses* as a product of schzophrenia' as 'nothing would be gained by this label'.[25] Like the writer of the letter, then, Jung does not diagnose schizophrenia in the author; unlike him, he goes on to discover the originality and value of the work in question instead of assuming that a style reminiscent of schizophrenic expression is *ipso facto* worthless.

Secondly, my own experience was proof to me that the effect of Beckett's plays can be salutary, forcing one to stop blinding oneself to existential and religious problems and to resolve them. However, it seemed undeniable that Beckett's plays depict a deeply-rooted neurotic disturbance of the type that he has always shown interest in. Furthermore, it seemed clear that this disturbance can be transmitted to spectators, perhaps because of the deep emotional relationship that often exists between spectators and the visible creatures of illusion on the stage.

Having accepted these probabilities, one is faced with several interesting questions: how is the effect transmitted? How is a mental state made dramatic? What exactly is the effect (exhilarating? disturbing? depressing?)? What do spectators themselves think about being exposed to this disturbing experience? And then, what is the status of this experience? Is it simply the twentieth-century equivalent of the Sunday afternoon entertainment in Elizabethan times—looking at the inmates of Bedlam? Or has it the function of tragedy, which used to be, as Simon Lesser puts it in *Fiction and the Unconscious*, to face and work through the aspects of our own nature and the human predicament which are most likely to arouse anxiety? How is it, one may finally ask, that such a private affair as a dramatist's wrestling with his divided self can awaken a deep and generalised reaction in spectators?

The trap to avoid at this stage is that of attempting to psycho-analyse Ionesco and Beckett on the basis of the obvious confessional element in their plays. Ionesco himself has objected strongly to the kind of criticism that substitutes psychoanalysis for an attempt at understanding a work (*Conversations*, p. 46), and Jung has clearly laid down the limits of a psychological approach to literature in his essay on 'The Relation of Analytical Psychology to Poetry'.[26] If the psychologist is not to violate the nature of literature (and religion) he must confine himself to the process of artistic creation and must not turn the artist into a clinical case. In the ensuing pages, therefore, the reader need have no fear that the plays of Beckett and Ionesco are going to be run up Freudian or Jungian flag-poles.

3 A Big Pale Blur in the Great Deeps

One of the disappointing aspects of human nature is that it so often does not seem to hang together properly. If drama – call it comedy, tragedy, or tragicomedy, it hardly matters these days – can help us to work through that problem, it will have shown its age-old therapeutic power has not been lost. As experiments with psychodrama have shown during the last twenty years, of all art forms the theatre is the only one able to *show* us (not tell us) the essential part social role-playing has in acquiring and maintaining a sense of reality, through the establishment of relationships. Sartre makes this the central problem in his adaptation of Dumas's *Kean*, the actor who feels more real on stage than off it. It was Moreno's great innovatory studies of psychodrama that led Eric Bentley to an understanding of Schopenhauer's word's, 'the drama is the most perfect reflection of human existence'.[27] That idea can be developed along the lines of social realism, of course, but let us pursue it in terms of theatre's ability to enact a revelation (rather than a reflection) of the ceaselessly changing, indefinable identity of the Self (which to Mrs Rooney of *All that Fall* is just a 'big pale blur').

Ionesco has said that he has tried in his plays 'to show characters who are seeking a kind of life, an essential reality. They suffer at being cut off from themselves . . . . The characters suffer from not being, they suffer from their lack.'[28] Nowhere in his plays is this to be seen more clearly expressed than in *Victims of Duty*, in which Choubert's search, deep down within his memory, for the unknown Mallot, is an enforced exploration in quest for his own self. Ionesco's own explanation

58

of the original inspiration of this play makes it clear why he called it a *pseudo-drama*:

> I did not want to write a comedy, or a *drame*, or a tragedy, but simply a lyrical text, something 'lived'; on to the stage I projected my doubts, my profound anguish, in dialogue form; I incarnated my antagonisms; I wrote with the greatest sincerity, tore my entrails . . . . They called me a charlatan, a joker.[29]

The play was Ionesco's own 'drama', then, fulfilling a similar function to that of psychodrama. But Choubert-Ionesco's search for true being, for ontological security, was fruitless. In vain is Choubert forced to slide back and down through all the selves he has been, in vain is his faulty memory stuffed with bread. For our sense of selfhood is profoundly shaken when memory cannot recall the past upon which the present self is built, as Beckett shows so agonisingly in *Godot*:

ESTRAGON: What did we do yesterday ?
VLADIMIR: What did we do yesterday ?
ESTRAGON: Yes.
VLADIMIR: Why . . . (*Angrily*). Nothing is certain when you're about.

Whereas Ionesco turned away from the problem of self as a major theme with the impasse of *Victims of Duty*, deciding to be a joker if that was what people wanted, Beckett has relentlessly continued the search. The year 1953 marked a turning-point in both their lives and careers. The first volume of Ionesco's plays was published, and he became the champion of the 'avant-garde' (a term he professes not to understand). Fame hit them both—but their reactions were very different. When success came to Ionesco, a sense of personal security came with it, and he no longer felt it essential, for his own satisfaction, to pursue the quest for permanent identity. His next two major plays, *The Killer* (1957) and *Rhinoceros* (1958) show us a hero with an undoubted sense of personality. Bérenger has a self—but this problem was solved only for the intimately related one of mortality to spring up, making a mockery of Bérenger's feeling of indestructibility.

We are not concerned at the moment with the overt problems Ionesco deals with in his plays, but with the connexion between his act of creation and the spectator's act of creation through his response. The most interesting point about his plays from this point of view is that some were written in quite a different mental state from others. When he was writing *Victims of Duty* and *Amédée or How to Get Rid of It* he was, he says, in a nightmare state, governed by the extra-conscious logic of the dream. Out of an initial image or series of images this type of play grows without will power or conscious effort. *The Chairs* grew out of the image of chairs; *Amédée* grew out of a dream about a corpse stretched out in a corridor; *A Stroll in the Air* originated in his dream – a very common one – about flying. Several dreams are externalised in *Hunger and Thirst*— meeting a person you know to be dead, the house caving in. *Rhinoceros*, on the other hand, was an assimilated dream or nightmare, with parallel levels of consciousness. *The Killer* was even more distant from the primary obsession which inspired it, because it was first externalised in the form of a short story, *The Colonel's Photo*. *Exit the King* is at the other end of the creative scale from *Victims of Duty*, a 'very wide-awake play' which did not have a dream as its starting point.[30]

No one with the least acquaintance with Freud or Jung will be unaware of the fact that dreams structure psychic disturbances in us all.[31] Even the retelling of dreams can transmit disturbance to some people:

ESTRAGON: I had a dream.
VLADIMIR: Don't tell me!
ESTRAGON: I dreamt that —
VLADIMIR: DON'T TELL ME !
ESTRAGON: *(gesture towards the universe)*: This one is enough for you? It's not nice of you, Didi. Who am I to tell my private nightmares to if I can't tell them to you?
VLADIMIR: Let them remain private. You know I can't bear that.

If retelling can bring out this strong reaction, of which Beckett is obviously aware, dramatic re-enactment can trigger off even deeper responses, as we shall see, when it arises from the timeless depths and transcends personal experiences.

Let us consider first the mysterious world that opens up to us when we see *Endgame*: prisoners in a room or – as it is called – a shelter. Both Clov and Hamm could go out, but they will not. Hamm is afraid to because 'outside it's death', 'corpsed', '*mortibus*'. We assume, therefore, that some eco-catastrophe has occurred; the Bomb, perhaps, or the predictable result of not taking *Doomwatch* seriously. But we also know that nothing Beckett has written can lead us to suppose that he is interested in exploring the social situation of individuals taking refuge in an H-Bomb shelter. The dramatic situation Beckett chose was simply a concretisation of his own mental state, another attempt at exploring and discovering the essential self. What is the connexion between this exploration and the situation presented to us in *Endgame*? G. C. Barnard has pinpointed the evidence, from the text, indicating that like *Waiting for Godot* to which it refers back, *Endgame* is another account of the warfare within the split psyche.[32] He restricts his analysis to the relationships between the characters: Hamm and Clov (two halves of one split self) cannot separate. Hamm, as a child, was forced into a schizoidal development by the callousness of Nagg and Nell, who destroyed his trust and sense of security. Hamm is an actor, the most schizoidal of all professions, demanding the creation of a spurious self, which is observed by the other portion of the psyche.

After all that, which seems to the layman to add up to a statement based on the text, on Beckett's known pre-occupations (a factor that many critics forget), and a psychological knowledge that is no doubt sound (though possibly misapplied), after all that one may still ask that infuriating but often devastating question, 'So what?'

Surely the more important relationship to be explained by this kind of analysis is the one between the skull-like room with its grey-matter-toned light, and *the world outside*? In a paper published in 1961 entitled 'The Schizophrenic Child's Reaction to Time and Space',[33] we are told how frightened the schizophrenic child is by boundless, open, inarticulated spaces. Some kind of nameless terror takes hold of him. The terror of endlessness in space is repeated in the face of unlimited, indeterminate time (or eternity). Not only in the mentally ill, but in men of great imagination and achievement, this experience of the terror of the nothingness of space is very marked. Igor Stravinsky, for example, wrote:

> My freedom thus consists in my moving about within the narrow frame that I have assigned myself for each one of my undertakings . . . my freedom will be so much more meaningful the more narrowly I limit my field of action and the more I surround myself with obstacles. Whatever diminishes constraint diminishes strength.[34]

The phenomenon of the sense of infinitude was studied by Freud under the term *repetition:* it has no boundaries (or is purely repetitive), moving nowhere. There is hardly need to point out the importance of repetition in the formal structure of Beckett's plays. They are virtually unending and indecisive—but they are the contrary of shapeless. 'It's the shape that matters', said Beckett, who compensates artistically for the shapelessness of the universe, in order to preserve his sense of existence.

Hamm's anguish when he is not able to orientate himself exactly even within his narrow field of action (within the shelter) is revealed by his panicking need to know he is in the *centre* and to feel the limits established by the walls. It is obvious that Hamm's inability to move outside the bounds of the articulated space formed by the refuge has nothing to do with conditions outside—if Clov can talk about leaving, then it must be habitable out there. Hamm can explore no further than the boundaries of his own enclosed space because he is cut off from the reality beyond. But as he himself points out, the walls are hollow—there is nothing solid about them. His protection is precarious. Endlessness, or what Plato termed 'the unlimited', may invade Hamm's existence at any time. Even if one views this as a simple case of agoraphobia (taking into account the fact that a blind person suffering from this condition can obtain assurance of being protected from endlessness only by the sense of touch), Hamm's anguish is seen to be closely connected with that of Vladimir, Estragon, and Winnie, namely, it is a symptom of ontological insecurity, fear of the anonymity of the outside, fear of fading away and losing significance if deprived of the close presence of familiar things or a familiar person. Let us compare what we know about him with the description given by R. D. Laing of a woman who developed agoraphobia:[35]

> Her longing was always to be important and significant *to someone else*. There always had to be someone else. Preferably she wanted to be loved and admired, but, if not, then to be hated was much to be preferred to being unnoticed. She wanted to be *significant* to someone else in whatever capacity, in contrast to her abiding memory of herself as a child that she did not really matter to her parents. . . .

Hamm's childhood experience, and his adult fears, are very similar, but if one says sagely that he is suffering from a lack of ontological autonomy, one is on the wrong level, for there is a great deal of difference between ontological insecurity and a *basic existential position of ontological insecurity*.[36] The former is of interest to psychiatrists, the latter is a worldview in which knowledge of the existence of evil is not balanced by knowledge of (or a sense of) a strong, healthy and self-validating personal identity. Lionel Trilling has contrasted Shakespeare and Keats with Kafka in terms of their totally opposed world-view[37]—'the captains and kings and lovers and clowns of Shakespeare are alive and complete before they die. In Kafka, long before the sentence is executed, even long before the malign legal process is even instituted, something terrible has been done to the accused.' R. D. Laing (id.) takes Trilling's comparison further and applies it to Beckett, with whom one enters a world in which there is no contradictory sense of the self in its 'health and validity' to mitigate the despair, terror, and boredom of existence. In such a way, the two tramps who wait for Godot are condemned to live:

ESTRAGON: We always find something, eh, Didi, to give us the impression that we exist?

VLADIMIR: (*impatiently*): Yes, yes, we're magicians. But let us persevere in what we have resolved, before we forget.

Terror and boredom, yes; but despair? That is begging the question, for Estragon and Vladimir do resolutely persevere in their endless vigil for help from the outside. Even in *Endgame*, a much harsher play than *Waiting for Godot*, to assume that the ultimate message is one of despair is to ignore the other connexion with the outside, that is, between the other half of the split psyche, Clov, and the Boy, who in the French version is given overtones of the risen Christ:

CLOV: Looks like a small boy!

HAMM: Occupation?

CLOV: What?

HAMM (*violently*): What's he doing?

CLOV (*the same*): I don't know what he's doing! What small boys used to do . . . He looks as if he's sitting on the ground leaning against something.

HAMM: The stone removed. Your sight's improving. I suppose he's looking at the house, with eyes like a dying Moses . . .

CLOV: I don't know what he's looking at! His navel. Or thereabouts.

The mystical allusions to the Saviour in this original published version are quite significant in relation to the description given by M. A. Sèchehaye, in her book on *Symbolic Realization* (1961), of the treatment of schizophrenics. She firmly emphasises the extraordinary relation of the inside to the outside thus: the growth of a new interior life (and the healing that comes with it) must come from the dynamism created by the emotional acceptance of help from the outside, from a person who is another reality. We know that Hamm's childhood dependence on his parents was traumatically shattered by their callousness.

The natural consequences are his own callousness and inability to accept help graciously. Not so with Clov, whose instinct is to go to the outside and meet the symbol of help (his first reaction is to go and kill the boy with the gaff, but only because he thinks this is what Hamm would want). The religious overtones need not surprise us. This is a pelagian situation when viewed in a theological light: Hamm's vehement denial of God's existence (because there is no immediate response to their prayer), is an affirmation of his self-sufficiency and ability to rely on human will alone. He even tells Clov that he does not need him any more. But *we* see him, from the outside, as very dependent and vulnerable, merely blinding himself to his need for help from the outside. Clov, being more clear-sighted (with improving vision) is willing to accept the need they both share, whilst Hamm tries to transcend the need by performing the physically unnecessary act of shutting it out of sight with his handkerchief.

The action of *Endgame* is a much more thinly veiled psychic exploration than *Waiting for Godot*. It states the problem more brutally, less sentimentally, more tersely and economically than the earlier play, which had already exploited the problem of dependence on outside help in a very obvious metaphor. Whereas in *Endgame* the absence of meaning is treated as a bitter joke by Clov, in *Godot* it is a source of anguish for Vladimir and Estragon. They long for the unwitnessed witness who will give them reality. They do their best for each other, but it is hard going.

The fact that *Waiting for Godot* takes place in the open air in the middle of nowhere should not blind us to the fact that, like *Endgame*, it is an exploration of the fear of endlessness that is associated with, but not by any means restricted to, schizophrenics. Anyone who has been caught in a deep fog, or lost in a dense forest, will have a good idea of the sense of panic that threatens when the space around us has become endless and indeterminate, when all sense of direction and locality is lost, when we fear that if we stray from where we are we might end by being even more out of touch in an endless search for the way out. For Didi and Gogo this fear is as yet but a reluctance to move away from the central point of orientation – the tree – and a panic-stricken running back if they do stray from it (except at night when, as in sleep, they move off to their separate habitats of consciousness). Because Didi and Gogo are both fairly mobile, their range of choice of action is greater than that of the Hamm-Clov pseudo-couple. But the additional freedom of choice places them in a vicious double bind situation: they need help from another who witholds it. Conversely, they want to go away and be independent, but are afraid they will miss the chance of help from 'the outside' if they move from the tree. The cyclic urgency of this double-bind, which psychoanalysts regard as one of the most destructive weapons against the human mind, and a very efficient instrument of confusion, is revealed in the basic repeated leitmotif:

ESTRAGON: Let's go.
VLADIMIR: We can't.
ESTRAGON: Why not?
VLADIMIR: We're waiting for Godot.

The French version, that is to say, the original one written in 1949–50, continues with Estragon saying, 'C'est vrai.' When Beckett wrote the English version he made Estragon's response not 'that's true', but a single utterance, 'Ah!', which is differently interpreted with every new production. Small as it seems in print, it is an important exclamation, because it expresses the utter confusion and exasperation created by the double-bind. In the 1971 production at the Nottingham Playhouse (directed by Peter O'Toole, who also played Vladimir), Estragon (Donal McCann) exclaimed his 'Ah!' with the accompaniment of a niggling little bite at his thumb. The suppressed fury was rather too restrained to come over. Bert Lahr, that great American comic who played the first trans-atlantic Estragon in 1956, worked it out this way: 'I never changed a word of the text; but I put in business . . . like saying

"Aaah!" The reaction was in the text, but not the way I did it—with the pointed finger, as much as to say, "I do understand, but I don't."[38] Kenneth Tynan described this (in *Curtains*) as 'an "Ah" of comprehension which betokens its exact opposite, a totality of blankest ignorance'. That was clever, and dramatically intuitive, but the 'Ah' of Alfred Lynch in what I would call the most authentic production in England (at the Royal Court Theatre in 1965, supervised by Beckett) was much nearer the double-bind reaction. It was *exasperated.* And this is precisely one of the differences between the 1953 and the 1965 Faber editions of *Godot:* the reaction is specified in the latter as 'despairingly'. This is the despair – the utter hopelessness – created by a situation that cannot be solved without intervention by an external factor: call it Godot.

It is now a cliché to say that Didi and Gogo are two halves of the split psyche. G. C. Barnard (op. cit., p. 94) goes further than that, and sees in Pozzo and Lucky 'a much more radical split'. His evidence is based on Pozzo's words: 'Beauty, grace, truth of the first water, I knew they were all beyond me. So I took a knock.' What was this knock, asks Mr Barnard? He replies that

> clearly it was the onset of a schizophrenic split in which the imaginative part of himself, the function which William Blake called the Poetic Genius, was shut off and made into a feeble inner self, while the remainder of the ego built up a pseudo-self which was occupied with material prosperity. As time went on the pseudo-self grew more and more domineering . . . the inner self became more unreal and impoverished. . . .

And so on for another half-paragraph.

I have quoted at length because we have here a salutary example of what can happen when enthusiasm makes one elaborate a theory without checking the basic data: the 'knock' that Mr Barnard sees as the onset of this schizophrenic split was not a psychological aberration. It was a typographical one—a simple printer's error in the (first) Faber edition, which was corrected in the 1965 edition. The French (Editions de Minuit) and American (Grove Press) editions always had it right: it was a *knouk* ('knook') that Pozzo took. Although I was sure everyone must know what a knook was (except me), I ventured to ask Mr Beckett what it was. His answer was simple. 'Knouk: a word invented by me.'

Any of us could have made Mr Barnard's mistake in a moment of distraction, but one may wonder if this is a very helpful approach to understanding the meaning of *Waiting for Godot*. One cannot treat and analyse dramatic or fictional characters as though they were complete human entities. They are psychologically interesting only in so far as they form part of an overall image and structure which came from the writer's unconscious depths and which, for reasons unknown but time will tell, create a responding vibration within those who complete the creative circuit. 'The poet of excellence', wrote Diderot, 'is the one who has an effect which lasts within me for a long time.' Clearly some attempt must be made to distinguish between the ephemeral emotions roused by the plays we are dealing with, and the long-term effects in depth.

Hugh Hunt has suggested that in *Waiting for Godot* 'we are transfixed in a nightmare state of absorption, in which emotions, vaguely recognisable, appear to reveal truths below the surface of the common reality of what is happening on the stage'.[39] *Emotions, vaguely recognisable* . . . The essential point about the characters in Beckett's and some of Ionesco's plays is that although they can be looked at in psychiatric terms, none of them could be regarded as a clinical case without severely distorting the author's intentions in creating them. In this context it is pleasing to be able to bring together two statements by Jung and Freud.

> In general [Jung wrote] it is the non-psychological novel that offers the richest opportunities for psychological elucidation. Here the author, having no intentions of this sort, does not show his characters in a psychological light and thus leaves room for analysis and interpretation . . .[41]

Freud was equally struck by the ineffectiveness of psychopathic characters when presented in drama because they

> become as useless for the stage as they are for life itself. For the
> sick neurotic is to us a man into whose conflict we can obtain no
> insight (empathy) . . . [41]

A little earlier in his argument Freud has postulated that for
the spectator to feel that he is a victim of the same conflict
as the hero, the neurotic impulse must be so indefinite that
'the process of reaching consciousness goes on in turn within
the spectator while his attention is distracted and he is in the
grip of his emotions, rather than capable of rational judgment'.

The original impulse that stimulated the dramatic characters
and structures of plays which are, in Jung's terminology,
visionary rather than psychological or personalistic, has
been so little 'worked over' by conscious techniques of play-
making that there is never any attempt by Beckett or Ionesco
to express them in psychological terms. The psychic problem
is never overtly expressed, but it is constantly present in the
characters' relationships with each other and with the spectator.
Our relationships with Beckett's characters are particularly
complex and variable. The periodic injection of statements
that involve *our* sense of being (such as Winnie's strange feeling
that someone is looking at her: 'I am clear, then dim, then
gone, then dim again, then clear again, and so on, back and
forth, in and out of someone's eye')—the injection of that sort
of statement into a monologue or a dialogue ('At me too someone is looking, of me too someone is saying, He is sleeping,
he knows nothing, let him sleep on,' muses Vladimir) which is
mainly concerned with the trivialities of the *character's* existence,
has the effect of maintaining an alternation of tension and release,
a constant diachronic oscillation between the eternal and the
everyday, that the empathic spectator reacts to very strongly.
This tension is not simply an aesthetic response as it is with
music (as Bergson points out, this a short-lived response).
It is a response to an overall stimulus compounded of allusive

style, subconscious or spontaneous structuring, and transferred anxiety, which probes well beyond any individual
neuroses into the area of deep and generalised concern. The
psychiatrist may be struck by the similarity between this style
and content and the schizophrenic's habit of mixing important
things among a lot of deliberate red-herring nonsense, 'to
create boredom and futility in others'.[42] But what strikes the
dramatic critic about the plays of Beckett and Ionesco, with
few exceptions, is their ability to represent boredom and futility
with a moving intensity that demands to be explained.

4 *Dramatic Intensity*

Intensity may seem a strange quality to ascribe to a type of drama which does away, as Beckett's plays do, with the traditional methods of creating tension; a type of drama which occasionally arouses suspense or the hope of the fulfilment of expectation, only to let them die away.

In the realm of psycho-dynamic processes, of which response to aesthetic stimuli constitutes an important aspect, the intensity of a stimulus can be gauged only by the intensity of the reaction it provokes. As Arthur Koestler has put it, the work of art provides only the electrical installations—the current has to be generated by the consumer.[43]

Once one has convinced oneself that it is really the intensity of reaction or experience that one is attempting to assess and characterise, one is faced with two problems: the first is to find out how spectators react; the second is to evolve a working theory that will help in accounting for the degree and kind of tension created by plays written with a minimum of conscious control. To what extent is the impact upon the empathic spectator simply a short-term reaction to particular dramatic and stylistic devices, and to what extent is it caused by the fear of non-being and the ontological insecurity pervading the plays of both Beckett and Ionesco?

It is not difficult to find terms describing the qualities of Beckett's theatrical language that give it its intensity—economy, sparseness, purity, compression; allusiveness, synchronic and diachronic effects with all the wealth of ambiguities that divide the public into those who find them infuriating and those who welcome them as an inexhaustible source of new reactions and interpretations. The equation of means to ends reveals a degree of efficiency in Beckett's writing that sets it quite apart from the self-indulgence of Ionesco. If Beckett's plays have got shorter and shorter, it is because he feels that what he has to say can be expressed in less and less space. Would that all dramatists spared us in this way. It is impressive, for example, that whereas Strindberg needed fifty-one characters in *The Dream Play*, Beckett's threnody needs only four. This narrowing down is also an intensification; each time more of the non-essentials are pruned:

Waiting for Godot (1948–9) – four characters, all mobile but visibly disintegrating;

Endgame (1956) – four characters again, but two static and moribund, one chair-ridden and blind, the fourth hardly a long-distance runner;

Krapp's Last Tape (1956) – one old man trying to recreate his identity through his memories;

Happy Days (1961) – one old woman on the verge of extinction, trying desperately to keep her past alive despite the constant engulfment of present time;

Play (1962) – three disembodied beings in limbo uttering scraps of reminiscences. No action, no gesture, no facial expression, no relationship between the three talking heads sticking out of funerary urns;

Eh Joe (1966) – one old man who does not utter a word, listening to an inner voice, the reproachful voice of a woman who had once loved him;

Come and Go (1966) – a two-and-a-half minute playlet or 'dramaticule' showing three spinsters sitting in a line on a bench;

Breath (1970) – no visible characters at all. Only sounds, light, and a stage full of rubbish. The lights go up to the sound of a newborn baby's cry; a rapid intake of breath and gradual exhalation coincide with dimming lights. Then darkness again with the same cry of birth. Thirty seconds.

It will be difficult even for Beckett to compress the meaningless succession of birth and death more than that. However, even here there is not total nihilism: there is the final cry heralding another life. When he omits that, his message will be the impending destruction of the life cycle. If one compares this 'act without words' with his previous ones, one notes that what is missing – apart from visible human beings – is humour, his usual release mechanism for the alleviation of tension. Perhaps we should not be surprised if he does not find the joke funny any more.

In marked contrast to the narrowing-down in Beckett, Ionesco's last play, *Jeux de Massacre*, shows an enlargement of imaginative horizons. The epic (or at least, panoramic) qualities of Ionesco's latest cry of anguish about mortality are not foreshadowed in the early plays, in which all the echoes of life in the mass come from the wings, or are merely alluded to. The perceptible expansiveness of the Bérenger plays (*The Killer*, 1957; *Rhinoceros*, 1958; *Exit the King*, 1962; *A Stroll in the Air*, 1962), still held in check by concentration upon a central hero-figure, began to break loose in *Hunger and Thirst* (1964), in which the unifying hero, Jean, is involved in three very varied episodes. In *Jeux de Massacre* (1970) there are eighteen scenes representing many different social situations (in the street, in wealthy and poor houses, in prison, in hospital, and so on).

It would be interesting to see a double bill consisting of *Jeux de Massacre* and *Endgame*. It would be a long evening, but the exercise in continuation and contrast would be very effective. The master of the house in Ionesco's play (Sc. 3) frantically gives his servants orders to prevent contamination within the house:

> If you do not wish it, sickness won't get into this house. It won't touch us. But go on disinfecting. Carry on making sure there are no gaps or cracks and nothing is opening up. Everything must be shut tight. There is no longer any universe outside us. We are impenetrable.

It is all to no avail, as the master of the house falls dead almost immediately. We have only to imagine that Hamm succeeds in sealing off his house from the disease of death to understand

Beckett's point of view: there could be something much worse than death, an all but endless state of isolation and boredom about which there is nothing to be done. Our attention is focused upon a state, not upon an action, and is therefore that much more concentrated (if there are no production gimmicks to distract us).

The very first exchange in *Waiting for Godot* prepares us for the diachronic quality to which we are now so accustomed. The sudden change or transfer of sense from the physical to the metaphysical is made without either of the two levels becoming superfluous: 'Nothing to be done' is Estragon's reaction to his boot's refusal to come off; but Vladimir takes the reaction over immediately and forces us to respond to the much wider sense in which nothing is to be done about the human situation: 'I'm beginning to come round to that opinion. All my life I've tried to put it from me, saying, Vladimir, be reasonable, you haven't yet tried everything. And I resumed the struggle.'

There is an extended example of this contrapuntal technique in *Happy Days*. Throughout the first act, Winnie keeps picking up her toothbrush, trying to make out the words on it. Eventually, with the aid of her magnifying glass, she manages to pick some of them out. They begin so magnificently: 'Fully guaranteed . . . genuine pure . . . ' (this is repeated several times throughout the act). What is this marvellous substance? 'Hog's setae.' She knows what *setae* are, but she cannot recall what a hog is. However it is not until almost the end of Act I that she gets round to asking Willie for a definition: 'Castrated male swine . . . reared for slaughter.' So that is the basis of those high-sounding pretensions: fully guaranteed . . . genuine pure . . . hair of castrated male swine reared for slaughter. This is how we play with language: we choose another sound to represent an object and forget, blind ourselves to the real nature of that object. The point has not yet been driven home, however (the English version has a telling irony that is absent from the French version).

Willie's definition of 'hog' does not come until near the end of the act and is immediately followed by his reading two advertisements from his newspaper: 'Opening for smart youth.' 'Wanted bright boy.' We are left to make the connexion: the hog, unknowingly reared for slaughter, the smart youth, and the bright boy so full of hope and ambition . . . they all finish the same way. Willie's message of gloom is not communicated to Winnie, however. She is untouched by it as she is wrapped up in and protected by her preoccupation with her love-song and her prayer. This, then, is an example of Beckett's use of oblique reference and comic counterpoint at its simplest, and therefore best. Willie's voice punctuates Winnie's ecstatic words. Pure music with a covert allusion to the emptiness of human aspiration. Both their lines have gone alongside each other already during the act as unrelated fragments, but now, at the very end of the movement, they come together and make their point with deep and stinging pathos.

There is perhaps no better way of illustrating the essentially dramatic quality of Beckett's theatrical style than to compare the treatment given to the same theme by philospher, poet, priest, another dramatist, and Beckett himself. Heidegger stated the theme clearly: 'As soon as a man is born, he is old enough to die.' This is the cold, stark statement of philosophical discourse, that does not affect us very deeply. In the seventeenth century this age-old preoccupation with the sad fact, 'How soon doth man decay', was the source of a beautiful poem by George Herbert, *Mortification.* Here, the poet finds reminders of death everywhere in life, and relates them to the 'breath' of Genesis. In every verse breath rhymes with death: When cloths are taken from a scented box to swaddle infants, whose young breath scarcely knows the way . . . those cloths are little winding-sheets, which do consign and send them unto death.'

In the same century, across the Channel, the great Bishop Bossuet brought his distinguished congregation to a proper sense of its insignificance with the reminder that 'a cradle is something like a sepulchre, and it is a mark of our mortality that when we are born we are wound in a sheet'. Ionesco, in *Exit the King*, makes Queen Marguerite say the same thing:

> The lies of life, those old fallacies! We've heard them all before. Death has always been here, present in the seed since the very first day. She is the shoot that grows, the flower that blows, the only fruit we know . . . It's a basic truth. And the ultimate truth, isn't it?

Beckett puts the thought into the mind of the blind and stricken Pozzo near the end of *Waiting for Godot*:

> Have you not done tormenting me with your accursed time! It's abominable! When! When! One day, is that not enough for you, one day like any other day, one day he went dumb, one day I went blind, one day we'll go deaf, one day were were born, one day we'll die, the same day, the same second, is that not enough for you? (*Calmer:*) They give birth astride of a grave, the light gleams an instant, then it's night once more.

The fury, the indignation and the melancholy voiced by Pozzo take the expression of the theme beyond statement of fact by the injection of emotion and even anguish; but self-pity and flatulence are avoided. Indeed we can see Beckett's pitilessness in the way he makes Vladimir pick up the theme once more when Pozzo has left: 'Astride of a grave and a difficult birth. Down in the hole, lingeringly, the grave-digger puts on the forceps.' That *lingeringly* is worthy of Musset. It is curious that Vladimir goes on straight away to make his statement of faith (atypical for a Beckett vice-exister) that 'At me too someone is looking . . . '. Curious because it makes the whole of this speech very reminiscent of the last writer one would usually mention in the same breath as Beckett—Lamartine. The same thought about the transcience of life:

> Insecte éclos de ton sourire,
> Je nais, je regarde et j'expire . . .

leads on to this consolation:

> Dieu m'a vu! le regard de vie
> S'est abaissé sur mon néant . . .[44]

Admittedly one has to be careful not to miss the flicker of an ironic smile with Beckett. Whereas one knows that Lamartine had no doubt about the secure and comforting gaze of God, Beckett may be inviting us to see the sheer ludicrousness of Vladimir's pretention to being an object of God's all-seeing eye. His lines, and Lamartine's could be considered as commentaries (with either similar or totally contradictory aims) on the eleventh Psalm: 'The Lord is in his holy temple . . . his eyes behold . . . his countenance doth behold the upright.' After all, the very title of Beckett's *Breath* gives away his ironic intention in relation to Genesis 2.7 ('And the Lord God formed man . . . and breathed into his nostrils the breath of life'). Neither are we likely to miss the point that *All that fall* is an ironic comment on the preacher's text, 'The Lord upholdeth all that fall'—a message that is greeted with 'wild laughter' by Dan and Maddy. Or the point that *Happy Days* is the first half of a jolly song, 'Happy days are here again'. *Waiting for Godot* seems to be just a straightforward statement of what the two main characters are doing, but the same power of ironic twist is obvious to all who know the fortieth Psalm: '*Expectans expectavi* . . . '—'I waited patiently for the Lord; and he inclined unto me, and heard my cry.'

It takes a particularly ironic turn of mind to write a play depicting a bitter wrangle between disembodied solitary souls in limbo, and call it *Comédie* (not rendered by the neutral English title, *Play*). The attitude of mind we are dealing with here is made abundantly clear by a passage in *Watt*, in which we find Beckett defining three types of laughter —the bitter, the hollow, and the mirthless. The bitter laugh is the ethical laugh (it laughs at that which is not good). The hollow laugh is the intellectual laugh (it laughs at that which is not true). But

> the mirthless laugh is the dianoetic laugh, down the snout – 'Haw!' – so. It is the laugh of laughs, the *risus purus* . . . the saluting of the highest joke, in a word the laugh that laughs – silence please – at that which is unhappy.

77

This makes us see Lamartine's line – an insect hatched out of your smile – in rather a new light. Could he have mistaken what was behind the smile?

All this is part of a much more remarkable quality of Beckett's plays, that is, their infective ability to produce the opposite effect from that which they seem to be aiming at. If you summarise any of the plays you are bound to end up by explaining defensively, 'You may not believe me, but it was often very funny.' There is a constant interplay between the pathetic and the comic with Beckett. It has been said that they neutralise each other, but this is certainly not what most spectators reported in the survey of *Godot* and *Endgame* (see below). Almost all thought the comedy *heightened* the underlying tragedy.

We might be excused for thinking that the emotional release of laughter is provided in order to alternate with the troubled tensions created in the unconscious by the cosmic statements. But I have noted during many different performances of *Godot*, *Endgame* and *Happy Days* that several of the apparently serious lines are also laugh lines. Just to read them on the printed page, one would simply not guess there was anything remotely amusing about most of them. For example:

VLADIMIR: Never neglect the little things of life (p.10).

[It is ludicrously funny, when one sees them, that they should be bothered about the little things of life, in their situation, just as it is amusing/pathetic to see Winnie taking great pains with her toilet in *Happy Days*.]

VLADIMIR: There's a man all over for you, blaming on his boots the faults of his feet (p.11).

[This is unintentionally aphoristic, and can be contrasted with Estragon's deliberate aphorism, 'We are all born mad. Some remain so', which is a laugh line because it is a parody of an aphorism.]

VLADIMIR: One [of the two thieves] is supposed to be saved, and the other . . . damned.

ESTRAGON: Saved from what?
VLADIMIR: Hell.
ESTRAGON: I'm going (*He does not move.*) (p. 12.)

[This is a recognisable reaction, the way most of us shy away from an impending conversation about damnation that is going to bore us. But it is doubly funny because Estragon does not move—a detail some productions miss.]

ESTRAGON: I find this really most extraordinarily interesting (p.13.)

[Here, he is detached from the action, and becomes one of us. The equivalent line in the French version is extremely unfunny: 'J'écoute!']

VLADIMIR: But the other apostle says that one was saved.
ESTRAGON: Well, they don't agree, and that's all there is to it (p.13).

[Despite the seriousness and sanctity of the subject, we find Estragon's exasperation amusing because he cannot shake Vladimir off this tack, and has to resort finally to common abuse: 'People are bloody ignorant apes'. But shortly after this, it is Estragon who has the *serious* laugh-line. They are looking at the tree:]

ESTRAGON: Where are the leaves?
VLADIMIR: It must be dead.
ESTRAGON: No more weeping. (p.14).

[A key thought – death brings the end of suffering – and yet it provokes laughter. But no doubt the spectator is still thinking of the willow.]

VLADIMIR: Well? What'll we do?
ESTRAGON: Don't let's do anything, it's safer (p. 18).

[Self-recognition—no comment needed!]

VLADIMIR: It's a scandal!
POZZO: Are you alluding to anything in particular? (p. 27)

[Implying almost anything you care to mention is a scandal.]

POZZO : From the meanest creature one departs wiser, richer, more conscious of one's blessings (p. 29).

[Condescension epitomised to the point of parody.] Pozzo's homily on present times raises three laughs as he becomes progressively depressed by thinking about 'our generation'. Each '*Silence*' marked in the text is perfectly placed for each laugh, and Pozzo's final valiant attempt to find something good about the present generation provokes the greatest amusement:

> Let us not speak ill of our generation, it is not any unhappier than its predecessors. (*Silence.*) Let us not speak well of it either. (*Silence.*) Let us not speak of it at all. (*Silence.*) It is true that the population has increased. (p.33).

ESTRAGON : I'm unhappy (p.50)

[This line provokes great mirth.]

VLADIMIR : You're not going to compare yourself to Christ?
ESTRAGON : All my life I've compared myself to him. [*Laughter*].
VLADIMIR : But where he was it was warm, it was dry.
ESTRAGON : And they crucified quick! [*Bigger laugh*]. (p.52).
VLADIMIR : This is becoming really insignificant. (p.68).

[The distinction between 'us' and 'them' is broken down, as Vladimir momentarily detaches himself from the illusory world.]

ESTRAGON : We always find something, eh, Didi, to give us the impression we exist? (p.69)

[It is impossible to imagine from the text that this is a laugh line, a release from the pathos of Estragon's previous line, 'we don't manage too badly, eh Didi, between the two of us?']

ESTRAGON : Do you think God sees me? (p.76).

[He is standing with his arms out, like a tree – one of the Yoga positions, as Beckett pointed out to Alan Schneider – staggering on one leg. At the same time as he is imitating the crucifixion (in Peter O'Toole's production, he and Vladimir stand each side of the tree in a Calvary tableau, which is justified by the earlier attention they pay to the story of the two thieves) it is amusing to think God could interest himself in the likes of Estragon. His question suddenly changes the tone of the dialogue—they have just been doing their exercises, and standing on one leg began simply as an exercise 'for the balance'. The meaning is swiftly changed by Estragon's mention of God: to balance the physical exercises they are now doing a spiritual exercise for which the cross-like stance is merely a shaping-up, and the laughter is quickly suppressed as Estragon shouts out his supplication: 'God have pity on me.']

One must not forget the biggest and most serious laugh of them all—Lucky's speech. At the Royal Court, Jack McGowran made this excruciatingly anguished, and I thought this was the correct tone until I saw Frank Middlemass's interpretation at the Nottingham Playhouse. He managed to make it touching and hilarious, with absolute clarity of meaning. Some spectators told me they were embarrassed by the laughter here; but it was not cruel laughter. It was good Bergsonian laughter provoked by the fact that Lucky becomes a thinking *machine* that has gone wrong.

No laugh cues that depend purely on stage business, on normal comic devices and routines, or on particular actors' ability to draw laughter by inflection, timing, gesture and expression have been quoted – the above examples far from complete the humorous content of the play – since we are not studying comedy *per se*. One conclusion that can be drawn is that the emotional release of laughter was felt by many audiences to be a spontaneous reaction to

(*a*) the injection of cosmic statements into a local situation;

(*b*) a sudden change in the spectator's relationship with the action on stage;

(*c*) quick, undeveloped reminders that the situation of the characters is ours as well.

One feature of Beckett's dramatic style is very easy to imitate or parody—but extremely difficult to render on stage with all its potential intensity of effect: silence. The fragility of his style derives from the fact that it is composed as much of silence as of words, and these cannot be captured on the page unless one is able to stop one's eye travelling down the page at each '*Silence* 'and '*Pause*', holding the previous dialogue in one's mind as if holding one's breath. Some of the silences are – or should be in a confident production – very long, almost to the point of being embarrassing. They can afford to be in Beckett's plays because they grow organically out of the pattern of words. The structural function of silence, as analysed by the Polish poet Cyprian Norwid (1821–83) is that of a part of speech. The silent and the audible are a double conveyance of meaning, interdependent, with silence preparing the voice to utter the next phrase. Jerzy Peterkiewicz has suggested in his recent book, *The Other Side of Silence* (1970) that much of Norwid's intuitive argument applies to the plays of Beckett and Ionesco. In *Waiting for Godot*, he says, '. . . silences are an undercurrent of every dramatic situation, but they become a pattern of gaps almost visible to the audience when the messenger from Godot arrives for the second time.'

VLADIMIR: [Mr Godot] won't come this evening.
BOY: No, sir.
VLADIMIR: But he'll come tomorrow.
BOY: Yes, sir.
VLADIMIR: Without fail.
BOY: Yes, sir.

Silence

VLADIMIR: What does he do, Mr Godot? (*Silence.*) Do you hear me?
BOY: Yes sir.
VLADIMIR: Well?
BOY: He does nothing, sir.

Silence

The words are an echo 'poised' (as Peterkiewicz says) 'uncomfortably on the silence which may contain either the truth or the threat'. He discerns visible gaps inside the meaning which remind one of the crevices in Norwid's analogy between lyric poetry and sculpture. 'Perfect lyric poetry', wrote Norwid, 'should be like a cast in plaster . . . crevices must be preserved and not smoothed out with a knife.'

One is struck by the relevance of these remarks to the later novels of Beckett, with their cracks in the meaning. The dramatic force of these novels will be obvious to those who have heard the readings of McGowran or the dramatisations of Jack Emery, but the reason for their dramatic quality is made clear by Norwid's thoughts on speech and monologue:

> Speech, because it is speech, must be indispensably dramatic. Even the monologue is a conversation with oneself or with the spirit of the thing in question. It is almost impossible to think up a sentence so abstractedly pallid that it would bring no silence with itself.[45]

But how difficult it is to put this into practice on the stage; even with reverence for Beckett's text directors and actors can still fail to please some critics. Irving Wardle wrote of the 1971 Nottingham Playhouse production (with O'Toole and Donal McCann), 'every little canter between Didi and Gogo is followed by an appropriate silence for the black chasm to reopen under their feet'.[46] This is an intelligent reminder that to obtain a dramatic silence it is not enough to keep still and quiet, that it must be given the right value by the surrounding words. In this case, however, with reference to that particular production, I should say that the comment merely serves to warn us the judgment of a very sensitive critic can slip if he has seen the play too often. For me, the *tension* of the silences came over.

It is the words that punctuate the silence – the void – whereas, for example, in the Royal Shakespeare Company's production of Pinter's *Landscape and Silence*, the pauses appeared so gratuitous that the plays took on the features of hollow pastiches of Ionesco/Beckett, and one was more than once during performance convinced that the actors had finally succumbed to the soporific atmosphere that had invaded the auditorium. The problem was solved with acumen and simplicity: the order of the two plays was soon reversed, so that Peggy Ashcroft would appear in the second half and keep the audience there past the interval. One is relieved to see Pinter's masterly touch has returned in *Old Times*. For an actor there is nothing so difficult as to simulate boredom without being boring. For a playwright the challenge is even greater. David Storey's very Beckettian play *Home* is a good example of the tedium that falls when the writer's style lacks the economy and allusiveness of the *poet*. Even Ralph Richardson and John Gielgud could not cover up the rapid loss of density and slackening of tension in the text, despite its ingenuity, pathos and humour. With Beckett our attention has to focus (as with any true poet) less on what he says than on how he says it, for style and matter are inextricable parts of his word-structures. But even though his intensity is poetic and dramatic, it must not be assumed he is writing poetic drama in the conventional sense. The self-conscious literary poetry of Eliot's plays and the self-indulgent melodiousness of early Fry are a revealing contrast to the tautness of Beckett's style, and make us appreciate his ability to integrate forceful speech-rythms and occasional, well-placed flashes of lyricism and poetic vision. How we are taken in by 'poetic' lay-out on the page!

> I love order. It's my dream.
> A world where all would be silent and still
> and each thing in its last place under
> the last dust.

Clov's 'stanza' gains nothing from *coupage* and indentation, which would be irrelevant to the ensuing dialogue in any case:

HAMM: What in God's name do you think you are doing?
CLOV: I'm doing my best to create a little order.
HAMM: Drop it!

The true poetic power of Beckett's drama is not to be found in particular stylistic devices or imagery, rich and varied though these are. It is to be found in the overall pattern, which itself assumes a metaphorical value. Martin Esslin considers *Waiting for Godot* to be so powerful a poetic metaphor, so archetypal an image of the act of waiting, that the play provides an existential reconstruction of one of the basic

human emotions and situations.[47] Elsewhere, Esslin deals with
the connexions between the kind of spontaneous inspiration
Ionesco experiences and the structure of the resulting work.[48]
When the structures of the subconscious imagination are
reproduced without conscious interference, Ionesco maintains,
the result is bound to be in the form of structurally satisfying
patterns. A play is 'a dynamic construction whose elements are
in balance by being in opposition to each other'.[49] Ionesco
has stressed the importance he attaches to archetypal myths.
For him (as for Jarry) the function of theatre lies in the representation of the great myths of an age or the great myths of
humanity; but, he warns, this cannot be done consciously, it
must come from the uncontrollable and unconscious depths.[50]
The person who gave Ionesco advice about archetypal dreams
was none other than the renowned authority on primordial
myths, symbols and the history of religions, Mircea Eliade. Dr
Eva Metman, in her essay on Beckett's plays, has stated that
'dramatic art has always been concerned with man's relation
to the great archetypal powers which can determine his
attitudes to life'.[51] We thus enter the realm of structural and
archetypal hermeneutics.

What are the archetypal qualities of the plays of Beckett
and Ionesco? Can Jung's ideas help is to forge that difficult
link between the creative structuring of the elements of the
divided self and the empathic spectator's reaction? To begin
with, the relevance of Jung to *Waiting for Godot* is brought out
by the story he tells of an uncle of his who stopped him in the
street one day and asked him, 'do you know how the devil
tortures the souls in hell? . . . He keeps them waiting.' Jung
goes on:

> This remark occurred to me when I was ploughing through
> *Ulysses* for the first time. Every sentence roused an expectation
> that is not fulfilled; finally . . . to your horror it gradually dawns
> on you that . . . nothing happens, nothing comes of it all, and yet
> a secret expectation battling with hopeless resignation drags the
> reader from page to page.[52]

85

Ionesco has said that it is not, of course, Bérenger who is the archetypal image of *Rhinoceros*, but the rhinoceros itself, representing the primitive, instinctual state to which man could so easily return. In fact for Ionesco theatre is an exploration of a conflict within the author which reveals the monstrous nature that lies just below man's civilised veneer. Ionesco is convinced his monsters are not just private ones—if they were they would not interest anyone other than himself. They are universal. This leads Ionesco to believe that 'this is the area in which an author and his public seek one another and recognise one another'. However, the communion he seeks is radically different from the frenzied arousal of audiences that is the function of the atavistic theatre of savagery and cruelty (Artaud, Genet, Arrabal . . .).

Beckett's conviction of the existence of a universally malignant force shows itself not only in the monstrous Pozzo (what could be more evil than the Italian sewer his name is derived from?). We see it in the strange emanations from the subconscious which are to be found in the manuscript of *En attendant Godot:* what I have called hesitation-doodles[53] —distorted, complex, tortuous, grotesque forms, vaguely human in that they incorporate some part of the human body. There is one enormous monster opposite the last page of Act I; but the vast majority were penned when Beckett was writing the scene with Pozzo in Act I.

Such spontaneous non-representational drawings as these arise from the recesses of the mind, as we all know, and are of great interest to psychiatrists. However, one doodle does not make a theory, and the only reason for mentioning it here is that it is the only clue we have to what was lying below the surface when Beckett was creating Pozzo, and wondering how to end Act I. The monster he dragged up from below whilst day-dreaming serves as a signpost to us in our quest for valid reactions to the play. Comic productions, and the emphasis placed by some critics on the comic qualities of Beckett's writing, tend to make us forget that underlying

Waiting for Godot there is a deep sense of evil, of fear and apprehension. Didi and Gogo feel it: they are not just bored, like Hamm; they are on edge all the time. Their preoccupation with hell and salvation, and the Dantesque purgatorial undertones, show us how real this sense of foreboding is. In a relevant production it is transmitted to the audience as a form of tension that is more than just an aesthetic response.

This atmospheric tension is created in part by the circularity of the structure, which renders the idea of separation or alienation from wholeness through the relationship between the inside and the outside, as we have already seen. Let us put this in another way, in terms of isolation from infinity (Godot?), the dimension Didi and Gogo are longing to reach, freed from imprisonment in the finite time they have such difficulty in getting through. Their concern with the passing of time is the mark of their alienation from infinity, and they are kept conscious of the passing of time by its very circularity, expressed by cyclic events. Each cycle is separated from the next by each revolution of repeating elements round the immobile elements. As in *The Unnamable* (where Malone keeps passing before the Unnamable, going in the same direction and keeping him imprisoned within a circle of finitude) Didi and Gogo are regularly contaminated with finite time by the very events they welcome as diversions (the arrival of Pozzo and Lucky). Diagrammatically, thus:

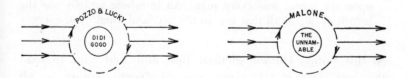

Didi and Gogo therefore exist in an area of dimension of *finite* time and are excluded from the infinite *within* eternity. This exclusion, this exile and separation, are perpetuated by the welcome appearance of the cyclic elements. So we begin to see the intimate *ironic* connexion between the repetitive structure of the play, and the overall theme of waiting for the end of time.[54]

The archetypal motif of *engulfment* is common to both dramatists. In symbolical language, this represents a kind of descent into the underworld. In psychological terms it is a sinking back of the libido into the unconscious; but that hardly concerns us. At the strategic level of *Happy Days*, *How it is*, Ionesco's story *La Vase* (*Slime*) and *Victims of Duty*, the structural image of engulfment is very marked. It is less obvious, but just as anguished, in *Endgame* and *Godot*, in which the preoccupation with the passing of time is so important. This has an effect which is explained by Jung's theory of the collective unconscious, according to which each individual is the scene of a permanent battle between mythical time (which saves) and historical time (which destroys).[55] In *Endgame* the original primordial image of engulfment has been eradicated in the final version, but the first version fortunately exists to prove what we should otherwise have surmised: it was, of course, the mythological situation of being swallowed up by the ocean, by the Flood. In the manuscript of the first French original version of *Fin de Partie*, Hamm made Clov read a passage from Genesis:

> And all flesh died that moved upon the earth, both of fowl, and of cattle, and of beast, and of every creeping thing that creepeth upon the earth, and every man: All in whose nostrils was the breath of life, of all that was in the dry land, died. And every—

At this point, Hamm silenced him and told him to read the rest later.[56] Ham(m), son of Noah, knows it all already.

However, there are some gaps to filled in, for we are quite capable of seeing a play about the Flood (Obey's *Noah*, for example) without feeling the slightest quiver in our deep consciousness. With Beckett, however, the creative urge

came not from a desire to write a Biblical play or to drama-
tise Noah's domestic problems; it could equally have been
(though one hesitates to stress it for fear of being hoist by
one's anti-psychocritical petard) the outcome of his well-
documented foetal urge.[57] Noah's ark is a 'kind of giant
uterus',[58] Hamm, having attained in his womb-like rotunda
something resembling the timeless peace of the embryonic
existence, refuses to be reborn, to go out. Similarly, the jar
in which Mahood is stuffed up to the neck (in *The Unnamable*)
and the ground into which Winnie is sinking, are archetypal
images of the uterus of the Great Mother World which
devours life and bestows it. The overall effect of the enactment of this type of creative fantasy far transcends the
neurosis, for the artist has transmuted it into mythological
situations and primordial images which are of the kind that
Jung saw are 'always characterised by a peculiar emotional
intensity'.[59]

Ionesco himself draws attention to the Jungian interpretation
of his two prevalent states of being, the one associated with light,
weightlessness and joy, the other with darkness, mud, heavi-
ness.[60] This expression of the separation and imbalance
between heaven and earth is, he recognises, neurotic, but he
insists that the real question is, to what extent is this neurosis
'representative of the human condition . . . or of a metaphysical
anguish, or else is the echo of psychosociological conditions'.
If the neurosis is representative of a generalised condition,
it becomes crucially important, Ionesco thinks, to explore it
in depth.

The connexion between structure and subconscious effect
can now be discussed in terms of Jungian *mandalas*. In order
to grasp the meaning of a visionary (i.e. non-personalistic)
work of art, Jung states, we must allow it to shape us as it
shaped its creator—this is called a *participation mystique*. When
Beckett asserted that 'it's the shape that matters' he was
clearly aware of the importance of overall structure in relation
to total meaning. His verbal structures known as *Waiting for*

Godot and *Endgame* are both characterised by four components and a circle, thus:

This is the exact verbal counterpart of the particular shape that Jung found had great fascination and therapeutic value for many of his patients –

– the *quadratura circuli*, which is 'a very important and influential archetype', an archetypal image of the deity, with the four quarters symbolising the parts, qualities and aspects of the One.[61] This age-old prehistoric symbol is a form of mandala (meaning 'circle') whose basic motif is the premonition of the centre of personality, a psychic centre-point which should be a deity, but in modern times it is 'the wholeness of man'.[62] A mandala is usually summoned up in periods of nervous crisis, and has the effect of reducing confusion to order (*but never consciously*). It expresses order, balance and wholeness, and is an instinctive attempt at self-healing. Jung got his patients to draw and paint, but Beckett naturally creates verbal structures in the medium that Moreno found to be so admirably therapeutic and which he termed psycho-drama.

In *Waiting for Godot* the central point to which all four figures are constantly drawn is the tree, the Cross (by extension of significance),[63] the symbol of the deity to whom Vladimir and Estragon both appeal ('Do you think God sees me?' – 'God have pity on me – And me!'). But these appeals to God, to the *central* deity, set him quite apart from Godot, who has many of the attributes of the old-style conventional image of God with a white beard. Are there, then, two gods? Why not? Beckett's view is a simple gnostic ambiguity: there is a demiurge who created this imperfect and suffering world, and there is hope for a Redeemer who may set all things to rights when he chooses, for reasons unknown but time will tell.

In *Endgame* it is Hamm who insists on being right in the centre—but Clov repeatedly displaces him, causing him great anguish. In Jungian terms, his wholeness is insecure, and he keeps on reverting to being just one of the component parts. There are a few lines in Jung's *Psychology and Religion* which seem very relevant to *Endgame*:

> The experience formulated by the mandala is typical of people who cannot project the divine image any longer. They are in actual danger of inflation and dissociation. The round or square inclosures, therefore, have the value of magic means to produce protective walls or a vas hermeticum to prevent an outburst and a disintegration . . . This state . . . is a much-needed self-control with the purpose of avoiding inflation and dissociation (p.105).

The protected dweller in the mandala is within a magic circle, a description which is even more strikingly apt in relation to what is clearly the next stage, after *Endgame*— *Imagination Dead Imagine*, with its two inert interlocking bodies lying curled inside a white rotunda.[64]

The Jungian critique of religion suggests that the search for a unifying symbol or factor *outside* the psyche can inhibit the realisation of wholeness from within. In Beckett's theo-centric play, *Waiting for Godot*, Godot is, of course, the absent unifying figure (and even if he is *deus absconditus* or *otiosus*, even if God*ot* does negate God the first syllable, he – or his absence – is still at the centre). In *Endgame* the symbol is the boy outside (whose religious and mystical characteristics in the French version, omitted from the subsequent English version, have already been mentioned). The mystical demotion the boy suffers in Beckett's rehandling of the text can be seen as a sign of progress towards an inner unity within two versions of a single play. This gradual unification of the split psyche continues in subsequent plays; indeed, there is noticeable progress made towards wholeness, not within the structure of any single play (for we hope and wait for a change which never actually comes about), but from one major play to another: four fragments in *Waiting for Godot*—two, plus two on the verge of extinction in *Endgame*—one in the *Act without Words* following *Endgame*—one in *Krapp's Last Tape*, *Happy Days* and *Eh Joe*. In *Lessness*, the ultimate in the undramatic, there is but one stoic figure, the only remaining upright, standing at last in unbounded endlessness, unafraid. All these are generic images of great power, very evocative because of the depths of inner conflict from which they arose.

If one turns from Jung as a source of enlightenment to Blake, a rather different picture emerges. G. C. Barnard (op. cit.) has worked along lines similar to those of Ionesco, in terms of structural balance. He compares the harmonious balance between the four functions of the psyche hypothesised by William Blake, with the four characters in *Waiting for Godot*. The internal psychological strife between the four giant Zoas – Los (Imagination), Urizen (Reason), Luvah (Passion), and Tharmas (bodily Sensation) – is given expression in *Godot*, Mr Barnard suggests, by the same warfare within the split psyche enacted by Pozzo (Tharmas, sensations), who has enslaved Lucky (Urizen, thought). Vladimir, the more feeling of the two tramps, corresponds to Luvah (passion). A state of alternating conflict and reconciliation exists between him and Estragon the poet (Los, imagination). This is certainly a curious coincidence which deserved to be pointed out without being built up into a theory. This analysis of the fluctuating relationships between the four characters in *Godot*, within an overall near-symmetry of structure, is more satisfying than Bernard Dukore's celebrated theory about Didi, Gogo, and the Backward Id[65]: Didi in reverse is Id-Id, and Gogo comes from (e) go-(e) go. More satisfying because the Blake-Beckett comparison is made in terms of the externalisation of a conflict within the author's mind of which Beckett could be completely unaware. On the other hand, for Mr Dukore's theory to work, we have to assume that Beckett *consciously* thought of Didi as a backward Id, and Gogo as an incomplete Ego. Ingenious, amusing, but quite unlikely. The theory again leads on naturally to the question *Alors?* or 'So what?'

This criticism is not applicable to Martin Esslin's analysis of Ionesco's creative process (op.cit., p. 131), for he is careful to take the next essential step, which is to inquire why the spectator responds to the plays:

> . . . aesthetically satisfying form is satisfying precisely because in being an externalisation of a conflict that has been solved it creates the precondition for a similar resolution of conflicts in our own mind—and this is felt as the harmony that is generally recognised as the source of aesthetic pleasure.

Mr Esslin's *rapprochement* of the psychological conflict underlying the themes and the spectator's aesthetic response to harmonious form is enlightening. However, his assumption that these plays represent problems *solved* is open to question. In *Victims of Duty* and *Exit the King* the obsessional fears that cause the conflict in Ionesco's mind are not resolved—ontological insecurity and mortality respectively. As we have seen, they are very closely connected problems, and Ionesco does not attempt to treat them in the corrective manner of social comedy. All that can be done with them is to express them by means of metaphysical comedy, which does not seek to rectify. The fact that the creation of the plays was not completely successful as autotherapy does not, of course, exclude the possibility that spectators might find them efficacious.

We have seen that there are some remarkable similarities between the kind of inner exploration that forms the creative process with Beckett and Ionesco. We have seen that a psycho-analytical approach to their works has frequently been made with varying degress of success and persuasion, and that the transmission of disturbance to the empathic or vulnerable spectator at a deep level invites discussion of archetypes and of structural hermeneutics. It may be generally agreed that although Ionesco's plays can be more dramatically effective on stage, in the sense of exploiting *grands effets* and traditional devices of sustaining interest by suspense, shocks and surprises, Beckett's plays are capable of eliciting a far deeper effect.

Catharsis is the term that has been applied to this effect— by Martin Esslin, Alec Reid, L. M. Rosenblatt, and the Hungarian critic Gábor Mihályi, for example.[66] Dominique Barrucand, in his recent major study of *La Catharsis dans le théâtre, la psychanalyse et la psychothérapie de groupe* (Epi, 1970) draws attention to the inherent paradox of the theatre of Adamov, Ionesco and Beckett, in which 'catharsis is simply the revelation of its own impossibility' (p. 129). But, he goes on, the very need to make this impossibility known shows a desire to transcend itself by demanding of the hero that he assume his own destiny:

> Despite the philosophical tendency of this type of theatre, pity and fear are what it inspires in its public, a public which is keen to participate and which more than ever, apparently, goes to the theatre in the hope that it will be led to live and understand the destiny of another self, will be helped to experience otherness and thus live and understand its own life better.

This is an Apollonian catharsis, then, distinct from the Dionysian tendency of – for example – Artaud, Jarry, the Living Theatre, Grotowski and Barba.

Barrucand's pages distinguishing between catharsis, abreaction and transference, written with sound medical knowledge to support them, bring a refreshing clarity to a subject that is all too often dealt with in a confused and question-begging manner. It is to be hoped that his book will appear in English before too long; meanwhile, his definition of catharis may be helpful at this point:

> catharsis corresponds to a modification of the structure of personality (with 'spiritual purification'), together with awareness of a repressed conflictual psycho-affective state which is re-lived, for example, during a dramatic performance or psycho-therapy (p.9).

Some indication of the complexity of this matter is given by the fact that Mihályi contradicts himself within a few pages. At one point he writes that the audience watching *Godot* experiences a catharsis, and on the next page he writes: 'the dénouement brings about not the sublime catharsis of tragedy, but the grotesque release of tragi-comical anti-theatre'. Bernard Dort appears to deny tragic catharsis in Beckett's plays on the grounds that 'Beckettian drama is but the obverse of classical drama—drama in which the decisive encounter will not occur, in which the conflict will not take place . . . . A desparately private drama.'[67] He sees Beckett's dramatic world as closed in upon itself, and yet two years earlier he wrote: 'Even more than *Endgame*, *Happy Days* calls forth identification and provokes catharsis . . . the horror is on the stage and is fully expressed there. It is not in the auditorium' (p. 266; written in 1963). For Gabor Mihályi it is this detachment of the spectator from the action that produces a catharsis in the audience. Conversely Ellen Douglass Leyburn has stated that many of the plays of Beckett, Ionesco, Pinter and Dürrenmatt

> present comic incongruity raised to tragic proportions and effecting in the audience tragic involvement and the tragic feelings of pity and terror. Because of the intense reality of these dramas and because they do raise fundamental questions, the mixture of feelings they produce is nearer to the old tragic emotion than that of contemporary plays of solely tragic intention . . . *Waiting for Godot* and *The Chairs* are both funny and terrible[68]

The danger of raising individual reactions to the status of general truths will by this time be obvious, especially when they are defined by means of what is, after all, despite its ancient respectibility, a mere technical term: *katharsis*. One can quote Aristotle and Nietzsche to show one is *au fait* with their theories, one can contrast Apollonian radiance with Dionysian onto-logical starkness, so long as one realises one is simply dancing aesthetic arabesques, philosophical fandangos. But the amount of actual enlightenment shed by this sort of activity is fairly small when it comes to the practicalities of theatrical response by flesh and blood spectators rather than philosphically sophisticated theoreticians. Arthur Koestler has tried to get to grips with reality, in *The Act of Creation*, by pointing out that if there is a replacement of the spectator's self-centred trivial preoccupations by his dormant self-transcendent potentials, which are then allowed to ebb away peacefully, then one can call that a cathartic experience. He uses the helpful image of *earthing*—a sense of individual tragedy can be earthed in man's universal tragedy, personal sorrow can be dissolved in a vaster feeling.

Our own little trials and tribulations certainly seem insignificant in comparison with those of Phaedra or Oedipus. The deliberate and inevitable unfolding of their fate released a redemptive force leading, we are told, to a tranquil restoration, providing the spectator ceased to identify himself with the victims of destiny at the pre-critical moment. Whether or not this prerequisite of catharsis justified Peter Brook's attempt to shock the audience out of the horror by means of the phallic send-up in his production of *Oedipus* is open to question. What is certain, however, is that there is no assertion of cosmic order at the dénouement of a Beckett or Ionesco play, no Apollonian comforting element—with one exception: in *Happy Days* one can say that lamentation is transformed into a song of praise. The possibility that Beckett wrote it tongue in cheek need not inhibit quite different non-ironic responses within us. Nevertheless, unless one is a Walter Kerr, even at the end of *Happy Days* one does not cease to identify with Winnie. Mr Kerr found that although he found himself moved by reading the play, 'in the theatre nothing happens to me at all'.[69] He does not say whom he saw as Winnie, and that is of capital importance. Certainly it cannot have been Madeleine Renaud—although by 1970 (when I last saw her) her performance was losing some of its freshness, this was not so three of four years earlier when Mr Kerr was writing. Even M. Dort, who has little time for Beckett, pays tribute to her triumphant ability to transform absence into presence, death into spectacular agony, words into discourse, by means of her powers of diction and gesture (op.cit., p. 266). It requires only Madeleine Renaud, he writes elsewhere, to enable the spectator to see his own image in the tarnished glass.

If we do cease to identify ourselves (as human beings subjected to the involuntary process of existence) with Vladimir, Estragon, Hamm, Clov, Winnie or Bérenger, then we are saying that *for us* the dramatist's tragic vision has failed to communicate to us the significance of the experience. The fault may not be his; it may be the fault of production or of our own unresponsiveness. Supposing the communion has taken place, can we say that the experience is primarily emotional, aesthetic, intellectual or spiritual? If any individual does hazard a statement, has he any firmer basis for it than his own individual response?

5 *The Spectator Speaks*

Sometimes we expect critics to do too much for us, so we cannot blame them if they often make unwarranted assumptions on our behalf. In his essay on 'Varieties of Dramatic Criticism'[70] Martin Esslin maintains that the dramatic critic functions as the vital feed-back mechanism for performers, who need an authoritative summing up of audience reaction, and he concludes that 'performing art like drama cannot exist without a reacting audience'. One might object that the critic is not fitted to play the role of a secretary minuting audience reaction, since he cannot 'represent' anyone's views other than his own. That is, not unless he takes steps to find out how a statistically significant number of spectators have reacted. It may well be true that drama is a dialectical tension between play and audience, but the nature of that tension cannot be assumed from an individual reaction, however experienced and refined it may be.

When I proposed a survey of audience reaction to *Endgame* and *Waiting for Godot*, the gap between the practical world of theatre and dramatic theory became very noticeable. Frank Dunlop thought that audiences would be very annoyed at being put through an examination when they had simply come to be entertained. Peter O'Toole was sceptical and uncomprehending. Another actor said, 'I feel too much about *Godot* to be able to write about it.' It would be unproductive, I felt, to point out that depth of feeling and failure to be articulate are not necessarily the same thing. If spectators do have strong feelings about a play, it was objected, they are incapable of analysing them; even if they do complete questionnaires they will not tell the truth.

At the first preview of *Endgame* at the Young Vic, I put my case. For many years now, critics have been telling us how *we* react to Beckett's plays. They think they are our spokesmen. They may be right some of the time for some of the people, but surely it is time we tried to find out how a cross-section of the public *really* feels when exposed to these dramas whose effects have been said to be akin to the catharsis of classical tragedy? A sensitive critic may try to gauge the feelings of an audience, but they are revealed only within a very limited range of manifestations—laughter, rapt concentration, restlessness, applause, boos, or walking out and demanding one's money back. Deeper emotions are quickly suppressed, tears are silent ones surreptitiously wiped away—at least, that is so north of the Channel and east of the Irish Sea. How can the professional critic, in his state of permanent theatre-shock, be expected to know what the average theatre-goer cannot articulate? I was not suggesting that *la critique de concierge* should be encouraged, for the value of discovering the opinions of the critically unsophisticated is clearly very limited. The questionnaires, therefore, gave little scope for value-judgements about the play or performance. Every man his own J. W. Lambert was not the aim; the stress was laid firmly on individual reactions to a particular experience. Finally, nobody was obliged to answer the questionnaires. Anyone who objected could simply tear them up into a convenient size and use them for whatever purpose, preferably during the performance of a piece.

It was possibly the idea of taking a little of the critics' power away that won the theatre people over to the survey. Even Peter O'Toole, whose devastating irreverence needs adjusting to, was quite affable about it in the end. Peter James, assistant director of the Young Vic, was enthusiastic and encouraging about it from the beginning.

The range of questions that can be put to a theatre audience is fairly restricted. They cannot be too abstruse or deep, otherwise the participants will become impatient and refuse to co-operate. On the other hand, if they are superficial questions they are not worth asking, and the more sophisticated spectators will not hesitate to say so. At best, the manner in which questions are asked – leading from simplicity to complexity – can be an educative process for participants who are not accustomed to formulating critical ideas or articulating responses. The only way to elicit answers at all, it seemed, was by progressive probing. It was important to have some guide to the character and beliefs of those who were completing the more searching second part of the questionnaire (see Appendix I), which had to be filled out one week after seeing the performance. To this end, therefore, two self-assessment questions were embedded in the body of the questionnaire, and were used as a means of classifying replies. These were Question 8 ('Normally I think *frequently/occasionally/seldom* about the purpose of my existence') and Question 14 ('I am usually a *depressed/happy* sort of person').

It must be said from the outset that the Post Office strike (which lasted for nearly two months at the beginning of 1971) played havoc with the returns, especially from the Nottingham Playhouse spectators, and the Young Vic *Endgame*. The numbers of returned questionnaires were as follows:

	PART I	PART II
Young Vic:		
Godot:	117	39
Endgame	41	10
Nottingham:		
Godot	29	29

These numbers, taken as a fraction of the total number of people who attended performances, are infinitesimal. If we accept that all spectators were seeing almost exactly the same thing, on whichever night they went, the returns can be thought of as fractions of fairly full houses (say 120 and 500 respectively). At Nottingham the questionnaires were unfortunately not handed out after performance, but were left on tables in the bar and coffee bar for people to pick up. All those who did not go into these places were unaware of them. In view of all these inhibiting factors, all we can do is to take the returns as indicating the response of 187 persons to Part I and 78 to Part II, persons who were interested enough in their theatrical experience to want to think about it and write about it.

The fact that it is not only the degree of intensity but also the type of impact made by *Waiting for Godot* that varies according to production is strikingly borne out by the run of answers to the question (II, 5) asking spectators to define the impact: was it primarily emotional, aesthetic, intellectual or spiritual? Whereas 53% of Nottingham Playhouse replies put emotional impact first and only 23% put intellectual impact first, the Young Vic production elicited almost exactly opposite results—58% intellectual impact and only 18% emotional. On the other hand, a large majority of both Nottingham and Young Vic replies found the play pessimistic, *and* thought Beckett is a compassionate writer. The vast majority, in both cities, considered themselves to be normally happy people (rather than depressed) *and* thought they had been more than usually pensive during the week after seeing the play.

One of the most striking results is that very few of the Young Vic spectators felt exhilarated after performance (10%) in contrast to 38% of the Nottingham replies. Why is this striking? Because the Young Vic production was a jolly affair played for laughs (30% came out feeling 'amused'). O'Toole's production at Nottingham, on the contrary, did not over-emphasise the comedy at all, and accordingly only 6% came out feeling amused. But the curious fact is that the more serious and reverential production had an exhilarating effect on a larger percentage of spectators. On the other hand, both productions had the effect of making people feel 'disturbed', 'sad' and 'depressed' to about the same extent: 25 – 30%.

Several critics – notably Alec Reid and Martin Esslin –

have claimed that Beckett can bring about in us serenity, calm cheerfulness, even spiritual liberation. This is true, providing one says 'can' and not 'does' bring it about. The survey result tend to show such reactions are very privileged ones; one week after performance 23% of the Nottingham replies indicated more than usual elation or happiness, and only 8% of the Young Vic replies did so (II, 12). Again, it is Alec Reid who claims that Beckett's plays lead (not 'can') us to a clearer knowledge of ourselves (op. cit., p. 58). At Nottingham 36% thought this true, 43% thought it false. If one thinks this is too low to make Mr Reid's statement a valid one, one should compare it with the Young Vic replies to this question (II, 22): 18% thought they had a clearer knowledge of themselves, and 63% did not. This is a very convincing indication of the power of O'Toole's production compared with Adrian Brine's. If only one had been able to put these questions to the audiences at the Royal Court production of *Godot* in 1965–6!

At both theatres there was near agreement of response to the question (II, 23) 'Which do you think is true: *Godot* is a dramatic statement of the wretchedness of man without God, *OR Godot* expresses the futility of pinning one's faith on a force outside oneself?' The second alternative was the choice of the great majority, and this correlated with replies to an earlier question (II, 21): 'The play has made me feel *either* life is meaningless *or* it is up to me to give life a meaning *or* if God does not exist life cannot have any meaning.' The vast majority showed themselves full of self-reliance (or *hubris?*) in their answers to this; and it says something for life in Nottingham that no spectator replying from there found life meaningless.

Although very few (10%) thought that *Waiting for Godot* or *Endgame* had an impact that was primarily spiritual, it is fairly clear that many were forced into a Camusian position of revolt against the absurdity of existence through personal action. Now, what about the worried doctor's fear that this sort of play can be dangerous and have an 'offensive, noxious, nihilistic' effect? Young Vic audiences seemed fairly evenly divided on this question (II, 10), but 63% of the Nottingham replies said it was untrue, and only 23% said it was true that there was danger for emotionally unstable people. The fear of unhealthy influence seems to ignore a common dramatic phenomenon which may be the basis of the moral power of the theatre; namely, the infective ability of a play to produce in an audience the opposite feeling to that at which it seems to be aiming. Robert Shaw, after seeing *Waiting for Godot*, wrote in the *London Magazine:* 'I don't know why so many people call it a depressing play. Beckett writes about suffering in away that makes me feel exhilarated—so that I must get up and go out and do what I can.'[71] It has been said (by Bernard Dort) that the primary function of contemporary avant-garde theatre is therapeutic—a very different matter from being dangerous, although a frequent early effect of psychotherapy is an increased instability on the part of the disturbed patient. Insofar as our deeply-rooted fear of the decomposition and the nothingness of the self is stirred by the 'psychodramas' of Beckett and Ionesco, any latent disturbance is very likely to be exacerbated in the first instance. As with all forms of therapy a single session has little or no long-term efficacy, either in the clinic or in the dress circle. When the stimulus to self-knowledge is a dramatic action, the process must continue – if at all – by means of the spectator's own meditation. In the case of *Godot*, the survey results are really quite striking in this respect (II, 3 and 6). No one – not even those who normally think seldom about the purpose of their existence—did not think at all about the play in the following week; an average of 73% thought about it now and then; and 22% thought about it a lot. Even admitting that they might have been thinking about the questionnaire to be filled in rather than about the play *per se*, we may assume that if the play had not been of sufficient interest in the first place they would have simply thrown the questionnaire away and forgotten about the play. The average percentage – 35 – of those who thought their view of human existence had been affected by seeing *Godot* was high enough to make one realise that we are dealing here with something much more complex than simple aesthetic appreciation or pleasure.

Both Beckett and Ionesco represent the anguish caused by the disappearance of one side of the cosmic equation:

the majesty of God + the nothingness of Man = the Universe.

For many agnostic and aetheistic writers the disappearance of faith in the majesty of God is compensated by faith in social progress and so on. But for Beckett and Ionesco, all that is left is the nothingness of man. When Hamm exclaims 'God—the bastard doesn't exist!', when the Old Man in *Jeux de Massacre* says 'Who can help us but God?—and he isn't there', these are not the joyful affirmations of materialist atheism, but the bitter complaints of disappointed hope. If man is nothingness it is logical to hold that all his works in the material world are also as nothing, so neither Beckett nor Ionesco can take refuge in these ideals. Ionesco expressly rejects political solutions; Beckett does not even consider them. The most we can do, they imply, is to make life as bearable as possible for ourselves and for others, however irritating we may find one another. Human solidarity and mutual help, so beautifully parodied in the second act of *Waiting for Godot*, are nothing so pretentious as an ideal for Beckett, but he does recognise them as a basic need of our mutual dependence. Ionesco's fear of massification, on the other hand, leads him to stress a more strongly marked dichotomy between the individual and society.[72] Hence, Beckett seems a more compassionate writer than Ionesco (his compassion came through very much more clearly at Nottingham than at the Young Vic—II, 4). Beckett's work is as self-centred as Ionesco's, but it is less egocentric. If he is a sounding-board for suffering, it is not just his own suffering. He paints a picture, not recognised by all but responded to by most, of man in solitude imprisoned within the time and space of a silent and unresponsive universe. Only the very brash or complacent can fail to react to that.

Finale

We have seen that as soon as one tries to come to grips with the dynamic problem of dramatic impact and intensity, one does well to abandon the static security of subtle but subjective comments on style and find out how – and if possible, why – people react to performances. No one would wish to claim that the plays of Beckett have an intense effect on most people; it is the empathic spectator we have been concerned with, and generally speaking this has been the kind of person who has reacted strongly enough to this kind of metaphysical comedy to take the trouble to complete and return (despite the postal strike) fairly searching and time-consuming questionnaires. So far, only the surface has been scratched; the process of inquiry certainly needs much refinement. The problem is that if one tries to probe too deeply, people become suspicious. For example, one would like to ask spectators, 'Did you find the play had the effect of an archetypal mandala?' but it is unlikely that many answers would be printable.

If the structural hermeneutic approach outlined above can be helpful in throwing light on what is indeed a very complex amalgam of emotional, aesthetic, psychological and religious responses, then we are nearer to understanding the dramatic density of Beckett's major plays. It would be very difficult to decide whether this is a cathartic experience, mainly because of the lack of definition, but also because audience response varies considerably according to particular productions.

It has been inferred throughout these pages that Beckett's plays can have a much deeper and more long-lasting effect than Ionesco's. To *prove* this will necessitate much more audience-response investigation of both authors' plays. However, it is possible to suggest a number of reasons why it is likely to be true. In the first place, Beckett's plays are less self-indulgent and therefore more dense and intense. Secondly, Beckett makes use of powerfully suggestive images rather than destructive parody and inconsequential fantasy. Thirdly, Beckett gets beyond obsession with death into a non-specific, mysterious world that holds greater fascination and haunting quality. Fourthly, Beckett's plays have a simpler archetypal structure than Ionesco's; in comparison with the classical purity of Beckett, Ionesco seems decidely gothic. Finally, although Ionesco raises hopes through the images of weightlessness and spirituality, he ends by dashing them to the ground for us. The redemptive force which is an essential part of tragedy is nonexistent. Beckett, on the other hand, does not impose endings at all in the traditional sense: we do not *know* Godot will never come, we do not *know* if Clov will leave, we do not *know* if Mr Rooney did push the boy out of the train, we are not *shown* Winnie completely buried. In all these cases it is the spectator who has to complete the action of the play and decide on its ultimate outcome and message. This is true creative participation, and it goes a long way towards explaining the dramatic response elicited by Beckett's existential exploration.

We have tried to show that what Grotowski learned from Meyerhold – namely, that a play is not a performance but a response, a reaction to a text – is true for Beckett's drama. Nevertheless, one must not be led into thinking that participation means the same thing in all cases. The participatory democracy of Brecht and Grotowski, the improvisation of the Théâtre panique, are quite alien to Beckett and Ionesco who dictate to the actors through the text and (by invitation) by directing. Beckett has shown to an increasing degree (recently with German productions of *Happy Days*, *Endgame* and *Krapp's Last Tape*) that directing is a stage of the creative act with which he can efficiently and legitimately cope, with his quiet and tactful suggestiveness and musical approach to words and cadences.

If it is true, as Diderot said, that 'the excellent poet is the one whose effect long remains within me', there can be little doubt which one he would have honoured with the term 'excellence'. The record Beckett has given us of his extended inner exploration puts him in the same category as Montaigne and Pascal, touching upon such basic human concerns that he is bound to affect many people deeply. His anguish at finding no pattern in the cosmos is transmitted through sympathetic performance to empathic spectator at a deep level of consciousness.

Both Beckett and Ionesco are frequently accused of having the effect of plunging people into pessimism and despondency. It is a matter that deserves our attention in this brief summing-up of their effectiveness in the theatre. The complaint was strongly expressed by David Holbrook, writing on 'The Destruction of the Erotic' in *The Times* (26 August 1971). Scientists still have an optimistic belief in man, he maintains, whereas the arts and philosophy are 'full of nihilism and moral inversion, blind to certain primary human realities which, in human biology, for instance, have never been lost sight of'. He quotes Adolf Portmann: 'Human life is a magnificent configuration of time in this same sense [*sic*], offering in its successive stages ever new possibilities of development and hence of living riches', and comments that 'one would never find a sentence like that in Beckett, Pinter, Orton or Genet'. Really? In Ionesco's short sketch *Maid to Marry* (1953), this exchange takes place:

GENTLEMAN: You could even go so far as to say that civilisation's constantly developing, and in the right direction, thanks to the united effort of all the nations . . .
LADY: Quite right, I was just going to say.
GENTLEMAN: What a long way we've come since our ancestors used to live in caves and gobble each other up and feed on sheepskins . . . The future of man lies in the future—it's just the opposite for animals and plants.

Ionesco is saying here just the same things as David Holbrook and Adolf Portmann, but it does not seem to ring quite true any more—such is Ionesco's gift for extracting essence of platitude.

In the week following Mr Holbrook's article that august body of scientists, the British Association held its 'annual orgy' (as the *New Scientist* called it), and showed itself to be completely divided on the question of man's ability to cope with the problems he has created in the world. Dr S. R. Eyre gave a paper on the effects of the world population expansion and the depletion of the earth's natural resources, and stated that a biologist would consider the rate of increase in births as a 'swarming stage' situation whose outcome must be mass mortality. He gloomily forecast that social scientists would be unable to overcome their faith in economic growth, that scientists would continue to put their trust in technology, and so the earth's last precious resources would be squandered and used to contaminate the environment. Finally, let us recall that the 1971 Nobel prize winner for physics, Professor Dennis Gabor, author of *Inventing the Future* and *The Mature Society*, argues that man's course is set for disaster, thanks to the indolence of the majority of people, and to the cliché-ridden unsubstantiated optimism of our politicians.

So much for the optimism of scientists. Some, it seems, are aware of man's limitations as a moral and intelligent being; it may not be altogether outrageous, after all, to suggest that man's cupidity, blindness, selfishness and prodigality may prove to be his most enduring qualities. The view of man expressed by Ionesco and Beckett is hardly reassuring. Are they to be taken to task for looking on the black side? It must be admitted that in an age when the tide of violence, thuggery, unrepented murder of children in the cause of political action, mass self-degradation through drugs and disgusted rejection of the consumer society by youth, there is a case for hoping some writers will be clever enough to persuade the man in the street (without boring him or making him laugh in the wrong places) to start emulating Socrates, Marcus Aurelius, or even Jesus Christ, instead of Caligula and Nero. But there is surely no case for criticising men of letters – as David Holbrook does – for refusing to allow the public to be complacent about man's moral stature. Where is the scientific evidence that man is a superior moral being now, compared to what he was at the zenith of previous civilisations?

For Beckett and Ionesco, carrying out their private exploration of the human condition through anguished self-interrogation and intuitive speculation based on shrewd observation of man's nature, the only evidence there is points to the certainty of ultimate solitude in an ontological prison where the only real patterns of movement are slow depletion and repetition. Their vision is prevented from becoming unbearable only by the fusing of opposites—pettiness, pretentiousness, brutality, egocentricity are presented with compassion, sadness and humour; their horror at the insubstantial pageant of existence is both relieved and thrown into relief by their acute sense of the ridiculous and of the absurd. Richard Coe has pointed out[73] that Beckett and Ionesco have in common the fundamental proposition that at the root of consciousness and of all Being there is a Void—but a *positive* Void which is the starting-point for a new lucidity and awareness of meaninglessness. ' . . . a play by Ionesco just will not work', Coe concludes, 'unless its underlying *Néant* is allowed to generate a positive significance' (p. 163). But how can this process take place? It is achieved by the *isolation* of what is represented on the stage from the spectator's world. As we saw in an earlier chapter (pp. 50–2 above) Beckett's plays also demand this solitary insulation within which, as in a play by Racine, for example, the norms by which significance is established in the everyday world no longer apply. Erich Auerbach wrote in *Mimesis*[74]: 'The tremendous impact of the passions in Racine's works, and in Corneille's before him, is largely dependent on . . . the atmospheric isolation of the action; it is comparable with the isolating procedure used in modern scientific experiments to create the most favourable conditions.' The classicist may regard the juxtaposition of two modern writers of tragi-comedy with Racine as rather pretentious, but Barrault, after all, did say that Beckett 'is the modern author who reminds me most of Racine';[75] Ionesco claimed, 'I aspire to classicism —if they call it avant-garde, it is not my fault';[76] the front cover of Raymond Williams's *Modern Tragedy* shows Estragon (with his trousers down) and Vladimir looking at a bit of rope; Walter Kerr, in *Tragedy and Comedy*, gets beyond the traditional classroom formula of tragedy to the domain where comic and tragic despair merge. It is no longer shocking to speak of Euripides and Racine in the same breath as Beckett and Ionesco. The classical hero who is the plaything and victim of the gods is not so far removed from the anti-heroes – the Bérengers, Didis and Gogos – who are the victims of hidden forces they cannot understand.

But where is the positive significance of all this? In the first place, the uncompromising stance of Beckett and Ionesco permits no complacency in regard to man's condition. It commands an honest appraisal of things as they are. Ionesco's horror of a fast proliferating world – in *Amédée*, *Victims of Duty* and *The Future is in Eggs* for example – Beckett's dislike of the reproduction of the species in *Happy Days* and *Endgame*, are legitimate reactions to the world situation as seen by Dr Eyre. The world is as full of Pozzos today as Germany was in the heyday of Nazism. We are just as likely to be struck down by a killer with a knife (who will be let loose on society again after a few years in prison) as Bérenger is as he struggles to reach the city of light. This is life as it lived. It is degrading and beneath the dignity of man's potentialities. It leads one to think, *pace* Adolf Portmann and David Holbrook, that perhaps Giraudoux was right when he suggested that man had gone past the point when he could have evolved into a creature superior to man. If one does accept the validity of this grim picture, is the only response possible to lie down and close one's eyes, to opt out, to drop out, to put up and shut up? As the

Beckett Survey shows, passive resignation is by no means the only reaction to be expected from this type of drama, which does not attempt to save the world, provide solutions, or point directions. Its effectiveness lies in its ability to arouse feelings within some of us that go far beyond and below our surface consciousness and social being without, however, resorting to complete fantasy with which identification would be impossible. *Rhinoceros* may put one on one's guard against conformism; *Godot* may instil indignation and pity; *Endgame* may inspire rebellion against an overbearing dependent relative or master; *Exit the King* may induce one to be prepared to accept death like the ancient kings; *Eh Joe* may prevent one's treating a loved one harshly before it is too late; *Krapp's last Tape* may make one realise the importance of avoiding living one's last days in selfish solitude thinking about the past; *Happy Days* can make one realise that today is to be enjoyed, for tomorrow may be even worse.

Above all, any one of the plays of Ionesco or Beckett may make one comprehend traumatically what a Godless universe means. Ironically, it is the Christian interpretation of *Godot* which brings out the absurdist vision most strongly. For it is the doctrine of the Second Coming which asserts that the world is not meaningless, that God's purpose for the world will prevail in the end. In *Godot* the message is of not one but two non-Comings. 'The coming of the Lord is at hand', wrote Peter. 'Mr Godot says he will not be coming', says the Boy. A quite legitimate response, then, after being subjected to this view of an absurd universe is to see with great clarity the need for faith in something greater than man, since the alternative is so demonstrably awful. When we are taken right to the very edge of utter despair we have no excuse for not realising what it means to say there is no God, no meaning, nothing beyond but horror till the end of time. There is no longer any possibility of our kidding ourselves about it, or pretending it does not matter. Of course, this is a disturbing experience; it calls our bluff. André Gide would have approved, for it does not leave us intact.

Notes

1. *Le Monde*, September 15, 1970.
2. Jorge Lavelli, *Les Lettres françaises*, September 9, 1970.
3. *Journal en miettes*, 1967, p. 92.
4. *Conversations with Eugène Ionesco* (ed. Claude Bonnefoy), 1966 (trans. 1970), p. 79.
5. Lucky's Peckham, where the 'eighteen holes tennis of all sorts' goes on, is mentioned by Broadbent in Act I of *John Bull's Other Island*: 'You'll find all that chaffing and drinking and not knowing what to be at in Peckham just the same as in Donnybrook'.
6. *L'Express*, June 1, 1961, p. 43.
7. 'Entretien avec Claude Cezan', *Les Nouvelles littéraires*, September 17, 1970.
8. *Les Nouvelles littéraires*, October 1, 1970.
9. John Fletcher, *The Novels of Samuel Beckett*, 1964, p. 232.
10. 'Beckett, c'est mon maître'—Arrabal to the present writer in conversation after a rehearsal of *Le Labyrinthe* by the Théatre Panique (dir. Jérôme Savary) at the International Theatre Club, London, in 1968. Ionesco wrote his appraisal in the programme of the Théâtre Montparnasse production of *L'Architecté et l'Empereur d'Assyrie* (see Ruby Cohn, *Currents in Contemporary Drama*, 1969, pp. 30–1).
11. Even Norman Holland, who does his best to transcend the pediatric details and move on to the process of transformation from fantasy to intellectual significance in his essay on Frost's 'Mending Wall', remains perilously close to the level of 'anal and phallic anxieties' that must make any creative writer cringe. It is remarkable that this volume of essays by various authors (*Contemporary Criticism, Stratford-upon-Avon Studies* 12, 1970) has *nothing* to say about drama (except a brief paragraph by John Fletcher).
12. See S. N. Lawall, *Critics of Consciousness: The Existential Structures of Literature*, 1968.
13. One of the few notable contributions to this field of study, based on practical experience as well as theory, is Theodore's Shank's *Art of Dramatic Art*, 1969.

14. 'L'Art et la psychanalyse, ou de l'interprétation au questionnement réciproque', *Critique*, December 1970, No. 283, pp. 1044-54.
15. *Théâtre public*, 1967, p. 249.
16. Ionesco says that a play is a play even without spectators, just as a building is still a building when it is empty. But what is the *function* of an unwitnessed play, and the *function* of an empty building (if its only purpose is to contain things, that is)? Ionesco does appear to be aware that value is derived from function, and not simply from the mere fact of existing, when he goes on: 'But all the same the play has been written for the public, for the public of its time; it cannot be conceived without the spectators for whom it is intended' (*Notes et contre-notes*, 1966 (Coll. Idées), p. 211). If by this he means 'the spectators of its time, when the play was written', it is a highly contestable statement. Modern productions of Shakespeare, for example, depend little on knowledge of the Elizabethan public for their impact and artistic validity.
17. In the collection of critical essays edited by Martin Esslin under the title *Samuel Beckett*, Prentice-Hall, 1965.
18. Notably Hugh Kenner (*Samuel Beckett*, 1961, pp. 155-65), Antony Easthope, 'Hamm, Clov, and Dramatic Method in Endgame', *Modern Drama*, x, 1968, and Robert Benedetti (*Chicago Review*—quoted by Easthope, *q.v.*).
19. John Fletcher, *Modern Drama*, February 1966, p. 406.
20. Cf. Th. Shank, op. cit., pp. 193-4.
21. *The Theatre of the Absurd*, 1961 (1962), p. 299.
22. *The Times* (London), September 25, 1970.
23. Published by Harrap in 1966.
24. Bourget's novel, *Le Disciple* (1889) stressed the ultimate responsibility of the philosopher and teacher for the acts of those who are influenced by his thought. Mauriac's essay, *Dieu et Mammon*, was a plea to all writers to assume responsibility for their influence on readers.
25. *Collected Works*, xv, 1966, pp. 116-19.
26. ibid., pp. 65-83.
27. Eric Bentley, *The Life of the Drama*, 1965, p. 187.
28. *Conversations with E. Ionesco* (ed. Claude Bonnefoy), 1966 (1970), p. 156.
29. *Notes et contre-notes*, p. 132.
30. Ionesco gives these genetic details in his conversations with Claude Bonnefoy.
31. *Collected Works*, xv, 1966, pp. 41-9.
32. *Samuel Beckett, a New Approach*, 1970, p. 101.

33. W. Goldfarb and I. Mintz, *Archives of General Psychiatry*, 5, 1961, pp. 535–43.

34. *Poetics of Music in the Form of Six Lessons*, 1956, pp. 66–9.

35. *The Divided Self*, 1959 (Pelican, 1965), Ch. 3, 'Ontological Insecurity', pp. 54–8.

36. The distinction is drawn by R. D. Laing, ibid., pp. 40–1.

37. *The Opposing Self*, 1955, pp. 38–9.

38. John Lahr, *Notes on a Cowardly Lion*, 1969 (1970), p. 278.

39. *The Live Theatre*, 1962, p. 156.

40. 'Psychology and Literature', *C.W.*, xv, p. 88.

41. 'Psychopathic Characters on the Stage,' reproduced in *Theatre in the Twentieth Century*, ed. R. W. Corrigan, 1965, p. 211.

42. R. D. Laing, op. cit., p. 164.

43. *The Act of Creation*.

44. 'I am an insect hatched out of your smile/I am born, I look and I expire . . . God has seen me! The life-giving gaze has been lowered upon my nothingness . . .' (*Eternité de la Nature, brièveté de l'homme*, from the *Harmonies*).

45. *Milczenie*, quoted by J. Peterkiewicz, op.cit., p. 70.

46. *The Times*, January 27, 1971.

47. *Brief Chronicles*, 1970, p. 222.

48. 'Ionesco and the Creative Dilemma', ibid., p. 131.

49. *Notes et contre-notes*, p. 212.

50. *Conversations with Cl. Bonnefoy*, p. 166.

51. 'Reflections on Samuel Beckett's Plays', *Journal of Analytical Psychology*, January 1960.

52. *C.W.*, xv, p. 110.

53. 'The Making of *Godot*', *Theatre Research*, vii, No. 3, 1966.

54. Both Beckett and Ionesco can be seen as working within ontological prisons. This is fairly obvious in *Endgame* and *Jeux de Massacre*: there is no escape from the shelter (or the prison in Ionesco's play), because 'it's death outside'. Similarly, there is no escape from the tree in *Godot*, because that would mean abandoning hope of salvation. One can see why Vladimir hesitates when answering Estragon's question, 'We're not tied?' Issuelessness is an important theme in Beckett's latest prose works, *Lessness* and *Le Dépeupleur*.

55. See Vintila Horia, 'The Forest as Mandala', *Myth and Symbols*, ed. Kitawa and Long, p. 389.

56. See Ruby Cohn, 'The Beginning of *Endgame*', *Modern Drama*, ix, December 1966, p. 321.

57. See, for example, Michael Robinson, *The Long Sonata of the Dead*, and G. C. Barnard, *Samuel Beckett, a New Approach*.

58. Jolande Jacobi, *Complex/Archetype/Symbol in the Psychology of C. G. Jung*, p. 158.

59. *C.W.*, xv, p. 81.

60. *Conversations with Cl. Bonnefoy*, p. 36.

61. *Psychology and Religion*, xi, pp. 71–3.

62. 'Concerning Mandala Symbolism', ix(1), pp. 355–84.

63. See, for example, C. McCoy, '*Waiting for Godot:* A Biblical Appraisal', *Religion in Life*, 1959; L. C. Pronko, *Avant-Garde: The Experimental Theatre in France*, pp. 26–7.

64. Cp. the two head-to-tail mandalas reproduced in Jung's 'Concerning Mandala Symbolism', Figs. 20 and 23.

65. *Drama Survey*, Winter, 1962. The theory is summarised in my Introduction to *En attendant Godot*, pp. xcix-c.

66. Martin Esslin, in his introduction to *Samuel Beckett: A Collection Critical Essays*, 1965, p. 14; Alec Reid, *All I Can Manage, More Than I Could: an Approach to the Plays of Samuel Beckett*, 1969, pp. 57–8; L. M. Rosenblatt, *Literature as Exploration*, writes (p. 260): 'Such works as Camus' *The Stranger* and Beckett's *Waiting for Godot* undoubtedly provide a catharsis for many youthful readers'; G. Mihályi, '*Godot* and the Myth of Alienation', *Modern Drama*, ix, No. 3, December 1966, pp. 277–82.

67. *Théâtre public*, 1967, p. 374.

68. 'Comedy and Tragedy transposed', reprinted in *Perspectives on Drama*, ed. Calderwood and Toliver, 1968, p. 183.

69. *Tragedy and Comedy*, 1967, p. 322.

70. *Brief Chronicles*, p. 258.

71. *London Magazine*, 1960, p. 35.

72. See the interview transcribed in Claude Abastado's book, *Ionesco* (Bordas, 1971): 'c.a. – Faced with society, you show the individual in a state of "instinctive" revolt. e.i. – The crowd is monstrous. Bérenger . . . is afraid of losing his soul or his personality.' But Ionesco's picture of woman's role is far more flattering than Beckett's. 'When I depict the couple, I tend to eulogise woman: I think woman is the custodian of serenity and love.' Beckett, like Flaubert, does not depict a satisfactory relationship between sexes.

73. *Ionesco: A Study of his Plays* (new edn 1970), p. 162.

74. *Mimesis: The Representation of Reality in Western Literature* (Doubleday Anchor), p. 337.

75. Interview with Carl Wildman, bbc Third Programme, May 1. 1965 (quoted at length in my edition of *En attendant Godot*, p. xxxii).

76. Interview with Claude Sarraute, *Le Monde*, January 19, 1960.

Appendix I *The Beckett Survey*

The Beckett Survey consisted of two questionnaires which were handed to, or left for, spectators at performances of Waiting for Godot *at the Nottingham Playhouse and the Young Vic, and of* Endgame *at the Young Vic, in 1971.*

Samuel Beckett's plays have been said to have profound effects on some people—effects as widely divergent as depression and spiritual joy. We should like to find out if this is a general experience or not. So we need to know what *your* experience is. Please help by completing as much of this questionnaire as you can.

PART I refers to your feelings *immediately* after seeing the play (either *Godot* or *Endgame*). Please hand it to an usherette as you leave, or send it in with Part II.

PART II (which is just as important) concerns your feelings *one week after seeing the play*. The address to send it to is given at the top of Part II.

If you don't want to answer all the questions, your answers to the others will still help our survey.

PART I (Please hand in as you leave, or send in with Part II.)
Please underline the words in brackets that apply to you.

1 I have just seen a performance of (*Godot/Endgame*).
2 I had (seen it/not seen it) before.
3 I had (read it/not read it) before.
4 I (want/do not want) to see it again.
5 I (think/do not think) I understood what the play was about.
6 I have (seen/not seen) other plays by Beckett (which?.......................).
7 *Immediately after the performance* I feel (exhilarated/depressed/sad/ bewildered/disturbed/serious/anxious/amused/angry/I want my money back/serene/happy/the same as usual (anything else?...........
....).

8 (*Endgame*) (*a*) the arrival of the Boy outside is a sign of (hope/
danger/doom).
(*b*) I think Clov (should/should not) leave at the end.
(*c*) I think Clov (will/will not) leave.
(*Godot*) (*a*) I think Godot stands for (Nothing/God/anything one
is hoping for/or..).
(*b*) I feel (sorry for/impatient with) Vladimir and Estragon.
(*c*) I (feel/do not feel) their problems are those of (humanity at
large/myself).
9 Your own brief comments about *your reactions* to the performance
you have just seen (go overleaf if you want to)...
....

Date of performance seen:..
Your age group (20 or under/21–30/31–40/over 40).
Please write your initials clearly here:..

Thank you very much. Now don't forget to send in part II a week from today!

PART II

(If you still have your Part I, don't change any of your answers!)

*Please underline all words in brackets that apply to you. You do not have to
answer all the questions if you don't want to.*

1 The Beckett play I saw was (*Godot*/*Endgame*).
2 I (handed in/enclose herewith) Part I.
3 I have thought about the play since (not at all/now and then/a
lot).
4 'Beckett is a very compassionate writer' (true/false).
5 I should define the play's impact: *A*. emotional; *B*. aesthetic;
C. intellectual; *D*. spiritual, in the following order (...........................).
6 The play (affected/did not affect) my view of human existence.
(If so, can you say how? – write overleaf please.)
7 The play was (optimistic/pessimistic).
8 Normally I think (frequently/occasionally/seldom) about the
purpose of my existence.
9 I recall the performance with (pleasure/distaste/indifference/
...........................).
10 'Plays like that can be dangerous for emotionally unstable
people' (true/false).
11 When I die I think I shall (cease/continue) to exist in some form.
12 Since the performance I have felt (anguished/elated/disturbed/
pensive/despondent/sad/happy) to a more than usual extent.

13 I like the play (more/less) than I did a week ago.
14 I am usually a (depressed/happy) sort of person.
15 For me the play was primarily (tragic/comic).
16 The surface comedy (neutralised/heightened) the tragedy of the situation.
17 I found the mixture of comedy, pathos and tragedy (worrying/effective/baffling/frivolous).
18 The play would have been (more/equally/less) effective if I had read it instead of seeing it. (If you think performance had a deeper effect than reading, please try to explain why and how [*This is important!*].............. go overleaf).
19 'My troubles seem so petty compared to those of Beckett's characters that I can bear them better now than before' (true/false).
20 Since the performance I feel more certain God (does not exist/must exist).
21 The play has made me feel (life is meaningless/it is up to *me* to give life a meaning/if God does not exist life cannot have any meaning).
22 Because of the play I have come to a clearer knowledge of myself (true/false).
23 *Godot:* A. '*Godot* is a dramatic statement of the wretchedness of Man without God.' B. '*Godot* expresses the futility of pinning one's faith on a force outside oneself.' (Which do you think is true, A or B?..............
24 I now feel I should (like/not like) to see the play again.
   I gave (the same/the opposite) answer to this question in Part I.

Date of performance seen: ....
Age group: (20 or under/21–30/31–40/over 40).
Please write your initials clearly here: ....

'A diversion comes along and what do we do? We let it go to waste. Come, let's get to work! In an instant all will vanish and we'll be alone again, in the midst of nothingness.'

So take this to the post now, while there's still time!

The results, expressed as percentages of the number of questionnaires returned (*see p. 100*), are given in the following tables. Some interesting reactions were recorded in response to the open-ended questions, and these are given in *Appendix II*. Initials and age-group are given where supplied.

GODOT. PART I

	Young Vic %	Nottingham Playhouse %
Question		
4 Want to see it again	56·4	63·3
do not want to	36·7	13·3
(want to read it)	3·4	—
7 After performance:		
exhilarated	9·4	36·6
happy	4·3	3·3
amused	12	30
serene	6	—
serious	29·9	36·6
sad	13·7	23·3
depressed	13·7	6·6
anxious	5·1	6·6
bewildered	12	13·3
disturbed	24	26·6
angry	2·6	—
want money back	—	—
feel same as usual	12	10
8 (*a*) Godot stands for		
nothing	3·4	16·6
God	21·4	6·6
anything hoped for	42·7	56·6
(*b*) Vladimir and Estragon		
sorry for	56·4	80
impatient with	14·5	6·6
(*c*) Problems are		
of humanity	66·7	76·6
of self	36·7	36·3
neither	—	6·6

Angels of Darkness

Question 8: Thinking about purpose of existence	*Frequently* 50%	*Occasionally* 30%	*Seldom* 17·5%	*Total* 97·5%
Question				
3 Have thought about it:				
not at all	—	—	—	0
now and then	32·5	30	17·5	80
a lot	15	—	—	15
4 Compassionate:				
true	25	17·5	7·5	50
false	15	10	7·5	32·5
5 Impact (first letter only):				
A. emotional	7·5	7·5	2·5	17·5
B. aesthetic	2·5	—	—	2·5
C. intellectual	30	20	7·5	57·5
D. spiritual	5	2·5	—	7·5
6 View of life:				
affected	10	12·5	7·5	30
not affected	27·5	15	10	52·5
7 Play is:				
optimistic	15	—	2·5	17·5
pessimistic	25	22·5	12·5	60
9 Recall play with:				
pleasure	45	12	12·5	87·5
distaste	—	—	—	0
indifference	2·5	—	2·5	5
10 Such plays dangerous:				
true	20	10	5	35
false	17·5	17·5	5	40
11 Believe after life will:				
cease	12·5	17·5	10	40
continue	32·5	12·5	5	50
13 Now like play:				
more	22·5	7·5	12·5	42·5
less	2·5	2·5	2·5	7·5

YOUNG VIC: GODOT. PART II—*cont.*

Question 8: Thinking about purpose of existence	*Frequently* 50%	*Occasionally* 30%	*Seldom* 17·5%	*Total* 97·5%
15 Play was:				
tragic	30	20	5	55
comic	7·5	2·5	7·5	17·5
16 Effect of comedy on tragedy:				
neutralised	10	5	2·5	17·5
heightened	37·5	22·5	12·5	72·5
17 Mixture:				
worrying	5	5	—	10
effective	45	25	15	85
baffling	—	—	—	0
frivolous	2·5	—	—	2·5
18 Reading/seeing: effectiveness				
more	2·5	—	2·5	5
equal	5	5	2·5	12·5
less	37·5	15	12·5	65
19 Troubles more bearable:				
true	5	2·5	2·5	10
false	35	20	10	65
20 God:				
does not exist:	10	12·5	5	27·5
must exist	15	5	—	20
21 Life:				
meaningless	7·5	2·5	2·5	12·5
up to me	32·5	20	10	62·5
God gives meaning	10	—	2·5	12·5
22 Clearer idea of self:				
true	5	7·5	5	17·5
false	37·5	15	10	62·5
23 Play expresses:				
A. wretchedness	10	2·5	—	12·5
B. need for self-reliance	27·5	25	10	62·5

YOUNG VIC: GODOT.   PART II—*cont.*

Question 8: Thinking about purpose of existence	Frequently 50%	Occasionally 30%	Seldom 17·5%	Total 97·5%
24 Wish to see again?				
Yes – same as Pt I	25	17·5	10	52·5
Yes – opp. to Pt I	20	2·5	—	22·5
No – same as Pt I	5	5	7·5	17·5
No – opp. to Pt I	—	—	—	—

14 Normally happy or depressed	happy 57·5%	depressed 7·5%	nil or both 15%	total 80%
12 Since performance:				
elated	2·5	—	2·5	5
happy	—	—	2·5	2·5
pensive	22·5	5	10	37·5
disturbed	2·5	—	7·5	10
sad	—	—	2·5	2·5
despondent	5	—	2·5	7·5
anguished	—	—	—	—
no change	2·5	2·5	—	5

NOTTINGHAM PLAYHOUSE: GODOT.   PART II

Question 8: Thinking about purpose of existence	Frequently 48%	Occasionally 41%	Seldom 11%	Total 100%
Question				
3 Have thought about it:				
not at all	—	—	—	—
now and then	26·6	30	10	66·6
a lot	20	10	—	30
4 Compassionate:				
true	36·6	33·3	10	80
false	10	6·6	—	16·6
5 Impact (first letter only):				
A. emotional	20	26·6	6·6	53·3
B. aesthetic	6·6	—	—	6·6
C. Intellectual	6·6	13·3	3·3	23·3
D. spiritual	10	3·3	—	13·3
6 View of life:				
affected	26·6	10	3·3	40
not affected	16·6	33·3	6·6	56·6

NOTTINGHAM PLAYHOUSE: GODOT.   PART II—*cont.*

Question 8: *Thinking about purpose of existence*	Frequently 48%	Occasionally 41%	Seldom 11%	Total 100%
7 Play is:				
optimistic	23·3	10	—	33·3
pessimistic	30	26·6	6·6	63·3
9 Recall play with:				
pleasure	40	36·6	6·6	83·3
distaste	—	—	—	—
indifference	6·6	3·3	3·3	13·3
10 Such plays dangerous:				
true	16·6	6·6	—	23·3
false	23·3	30	10	63·3
11 Believe after life will:				
cease	16·6	26·6	3·3	46·6
continue	26·6	13·3	3·3	43·3
13 Now like play:				
more	33·3	23·3	—	56·6
less	—	—	—	—
15 Play was:				
tragic	23·3	26·6	10	60
comic	16·6	3·3	—	20
tragicomic	13·3	—	—	13·3
16 Effect of comedy on tragedy:				
neutralised	3·3	10	—	13·3
heightened	40	30	10	80
17 Mixture:				
worrying	—	10	—	10
effective	46·6	33·3	10	90
baffling	—	—	—	—
frivolous	—	6·6	—	6·6
18 Reading/seeing effectiveness:				
more	—	10	—	10
equal	13·3	10	3·3	26·6
less	30	16·6	6·6	53·3

Angels of Darkness

Question 8: Thinking about purpose of existence	Frequently 48%	Occasionally 41%	Seldom 11%	Total 100%
19 Troubles more bearable:				
true	6·6	—	—	6·6
false	40	20	10	70
20 God:				
does not exist	10	16·6	3·3	30
must exist	23·3	3·3	—	26·6
21 Life:				
meaningless	—	3·3	—	3·3
up to me	33·3	26·6	3·3	63·3
God gives meaning	6·6	6·6	3·3	16·6
22 Clearer idea of self:				
true	26·6	6·6	3·3	36·6
false	16·6	20	6·6	43·3
23 Play expresses:				
A. wretchedness	13·3	10	3·3	26·6
B. need for self-reliance	30	26·6	10	66·6
24 Wish to see again?				
Yes – same as Pt I	36·6	36·6	3·3	76·6
Yes – opp. to Pt I	6·6	—	3·3	10
No – same as Pt I	3·3	—	3·3	6·6
No – opp. to Pt I	—	—	—	—

14 Normally happy or depressed	happy 60%	depressed 13·3%	nil or both 23·3%	total 96·6%
12 Since performance:				
elated	3·3	3·3	6·6	13·3
happy	3·3	3·3	3·3	10
pensive	13·3	6·6	13·3	33·3
disturbed	—	3·3	6·6	10
sad	6·6	3·3	3·3	13·3
despondent	—	6·6	—	6·6
anguished	—	3·3	—	3·3
no change	13·3	—	3·3	16·6

Question	%
4 Want to see it again	42·5
do not want to	47·5
(ought to)	2·5
7 After performance:	
exhilarated	2·5
depressed	22·5
sad	10
bewildered	17·5
disturbed	27·5
serious	20
anxious	—
amused	7·5
angry	5
money back	—
serene	—
happy	2·5
the same	10
8 (a) Boy is a sign of:	
hope	35
danger	10
doom	22·5
(b) Clov:	
should leave	45
not leave	30
(indifferent)	10
(c) Clov:	
will leave	7·5
will not leave	60

Angels of Darkness

Question 8: Thinking about purpose of existence	Frequently 30%	Occasionally 40%	Seldom 30%	Total 100%
Question				
3 Have thought about it:				
not at all	—	10	10	20
now and then	10	30	10	50
a lot	20	—	10	30
4 Compassionate:				
true	20	10	—	30
false	10	20	10	40
5 Impact (first letter only):				
A. emotional	10	—	20	30
B. aesthetic	—	—	—	0
C. intellectual	10	30	—	40
D. spiritual	10	—	—	10
6 View of life:				
affected	10	—	—	10
not affected	20	30	20	70
7 Play is:				
optimistic	—	—	—	0
pessimistic	30	40	20	90
9 Recall play with:				
pleasure	20	20	20	60
distaste	10	10	10	30
indifference	—	—	—	0
10 Such plays dangerous:				
true	20	—	20	40
false	10	40	10	60
11 Believe after life will:				
cease	10	20	20	50
continue	20	20	10	50
13 Now like play:				
more	20	20	10	40
less	10	10	—	20

YOUNG VIC: ENDGAME. PART II—*cont.*

Question 8: Thinking about purpose of existence	Frequently 30%	Occasionally 40%	Seldom 30%	Total 100%
15 Play was:				
tragic	30	30	30	90
comic	—	—	—	0
16 Effect of comedy on tragedy:				
neutralised	—	—	—	0
heightened	30	40	10	80
17 Mixture:				
worrying	—	—	10	10
effective	30	40	10	80
baffling	—	—	—	0
frivolous	—	—	10	10
18 Reading/seeing effectiveness:				
more	—	—	—	0
equal	—	—	10	10
less	20	30	—	50
19 Troubles more bearable:				
true	10	—	—	10
false	20	30	20	70
20 God:				
does not exist	20	—	—	20
exist	—	—	—	0
21 Life:				
meaningless	10	—	—	10
up to me	20	20	10	50
God gives meaning	—	—	10	10
22 Clearer idea of self:				
true	20	—	—	20
false	10	40	30	80

YOUNG VIC: ENDGAME. PART II—*cont.*

Question 8: Thinking about purpose of existence	*Frequently* 30%	*Occasionally* 40%	*Seldom* 30%	*Total* 100%
23 Play expresses:				
A. wretchedness	—	—	—	0
B. need for self-reliance	10	—	—	10
24 Wish to see again?				
Yes – same as Pt I	20	10	10	40
Yes – opp. to Pt I	10	—	10	20
No – same as Pt I	—	20	10	30
No – opp. to Pt I	—	10	—	10

	happy	*depressed*	*nil or both*	*total*
14 Normally happy or depressed	60%	10%	20%	90%
12 Since performance:				
elated	—	—	—	0
happy	—	—	—	0
pensive	10	10	—	20
disturbed	40	—	—	40
sad	—	—	—	0
despondent	10	—	—	10
anguished	—	—	—	0
no change	—	—	10	10

PART I

Question 7. 'Immediately after the performance I feel . . .'

(a) (GODOT, *Young Vic*)

[*Age 21–30*]: The same as usual (*G.W.N.*); slightly confused (*A.L.P.*); thoughtful (*A.G.*); nothing (*M.P.*); felt a bit sad, not because the play is sad in itself – it is not; in fact, it is exceedingly glorious and affirmative, but I did feel sad at the production in that I felt that it did not arrive at the height of affirmation which it should. Vladimir and Estragon exist in a relativist universe in which nothing is certain and, therefore, there is nothing to be done. However, they persist, they do indeed do things. That they can *do* in a universe in which there is nothing to be done is the great affirmation of the play – something akin to Nietzsche's great 'Yes' – which, unfortunately, I thought the production left me without (*R.W.A.*); confused (*J.A.C.*); purposeless (*A.R.F.*); hopeless (*C.C.C.*); contented (*G.S.D.*); exhausted, uncommunicative (*R.I.C.C.*); impressed (*S.G.*); grateful (*R.D.F.*); impatient to 'learn' (*C.L.-G.*); sympathetic (*G.R.D.*).

[*Age 31–40*]: moved by the rhythm – ebb and flow (*P.H.B.*).

[*No age given*]: thankful (*I.D.H.S.*); stupid (*D.G.S.*); stimulated (*A.G.S.*); relieved because I see a tangible plot (*P.G.F.S.*).

(b) (GODOT, *Nottingham Playhouse*)

[*Age 20 or under*]: impressed – I want time to think the play over and discuss it (*S.E.M.*); suicidal (*E.C.*).

[*Age 21–30*]: stimulated (*B.W.M.S.*); contemplative (if that's too grand – thoughtful!) (*V.J.R.*).

[*Age 31–40*]: made serious and anxious by the play, but amused by the characters (E and V) (*A.R.D.*).

[*Age over 40*]: resigned to my fate knowing I am alone with all mankind (*J.B.*); highly entertained (*M.H.G.*); made sad and disturbed by play itself, and exhilarated at performance (*J.D.*).

(c) (ENDGAME, *Young Vic*)

Age 21–30]: slightly disappointed *(R.J.A.)*; wanting and anticipating clarification at discussion *(E.J.L.)*; aware and somehow more alive *(A.A.N.)*; relieved that the end had come *(L.L.)*; under anaesthesia *(B.P.G.)*; sorry that the characters (and Beckett) cannot see anything in life worth living for *(G.M.H.)*; frustrated *(G.P.)*; bored and irritable *(W.E.O.)*.

[*Age 31–40*]: thoughtful, relieved at having the security of a personal philosophy *(A.L.)*; I think I have seen a powerful picture of humanity's soul-sickness *(D.T.)*.

[*Age over 40*]: exhausted *(D.B.)*; curiously related to the characters in their frustrations *(G.McL.)*.

Question 8(a). 'I think Godot stands for . . .'

(a) (*Young Vic*)

[*Age 20 or under*]: anything one is searching for *(P.C.)*; decision, or reason for living *(M.L.E.)*; something not defined one is hoping for *(N.C.)*; the ultimate perfection man is incapable of achieving *(R.H.)*; God and Nothing – we hope for God, God is nothing, we hope for nothing *(P.C.)*; external meaning in life *(L.A.S.)*; anything one is hoping for and cannot have *(A.F.W.)*; some key to escape/salvation *(A.R.M.)*; whatever one believes to exist without physical proof *(S.-J.A.)*; some definite purpose one feels life must have, without knowing what it is *(J.P.)*.

[*Age 21–30*]: release *(D.C.)*; life which the two tramps wait for but cannot go towards *(B.A.C.)*; eternity – something that never comes *(J.P.A.)*; God and man's endless frustration *(C.C.C.)*; help from themselves *(M.J.C.)*; the aims and goals of the individual within society *(J.G.C.)*; the infinite *(G.S.D.)*; death *(S.G.)*; an answer to existence *(E.J.)*; complete consciousness *(C.L.-G.)*; a projection of the aspect of one's personality on which one blames things one feels guilty about *(M.I.S.B.)*.

[*Age 31–40*]: meaning to life *(J.E.C.)*.

[*No age given*]: a raison d'être *(J.G.)*; it doesn't matter *(D.G.S.)*; God *perhaps*, but a purpose or value *(S.A.S.)*; need for a purpose *(A.G.S.)*; God – but I have doubts that one can make any final interpretation. This is intended to be left open *(C.R.G.B.)*; courage to change the status quo *(P.G.F.S.)*; the end of the world *(—)*.

(b) (*Nottingham Playhouse*)

[*Age 20 or under*]: life itself, maybe *(S.E.M.)*; futility of life

(*N.C.N.*); a God with a sick mind or a warped sense of humour (*E.C.*).

[*Age 21–30*): certainty (*H.R.D.*); that 'something' which lies outside our immediate physical or perceptive experience (*V.J.R.*).

[*Age over 40*]: one's relationship with God (*N.T.*); death (*L.H.*); the future (*M.G.H.*).

Question 9. 'Your own brief comments about your reactions to the performance you have just seen.'

(*a*) (GODOT, *Young Vic*)

[*Age 20 or under*]: frustration !!!! (*N.C.*); interesting essay on the pointlessness of life (*J.M.C.*); reading was much greyer. This is not so grim – makes more sense (*M.A.A.*); the play is an honest, logical reaction to life (*B.L.P.*); very muddled at first, depressed in the middle, glad at the end when they decided to leave. Felt this ended on a hopeful note (*J.H.*); at a different time I could feel different reaction to the play depending on my own mood (*R.H.*); any infinite search for a universe of frightfully relevant symbols is not what the play is about – it is everything and nothing. It is about two tramps waiting for Godot (*P.C.*); amusement, boredom during the performance. Perplexed interest and a desire to re-read the play (*J.J.B.*); I experienced a considerable amount of involvement with the characters, particularly Estragon and Vladimir, which I believe was a direct result of the setting of this production, with the open stage and the characters actually among the audience, as it were. I saw Estragon and Vladimir as being caught up on a kind of 'treadmill', habitually going through the actions of life day after day. Mr Godot, I believe, represents some form of escape from this routine: perhaps he is God, as there are several pointers towards this . . . or perhaps Mr Godot brings some other form of escape – but not death, for Estragon and Vladimir contemplate a suicidal death every day at the end of their routine evening. . . . The comedy of the play was in perfect proportion – neither over- nor under-done, blending superbly with the characters and the situation, the comedy having a great deal of pathos in it. One had the impression that Estragon and Vladimir had been waiting for along time for 'Godot' to come and save them from the routine of life, and that they were going to come again and again, it seemed, for ever (*A.R.M.*, who had read *Godot* but had not seen it or any other Beckett play previously); I identified myself mostly with Estragon. Although the play destroys the ideas of place and time and existence, it seems

very real and relevant to everyday life (*S.-J.A.*); most of it was very
funny and I think it's very clever to write something which is both
funny and thought-provoking – usually if you laugh at something
you walk away and forget it (*J.P.*); very satisfying, fulfilled my
ideas of the play on first reading. The play outlines the futility of
life, but one is not depressed about it, merely resigned (*P.A.H.*).

[*Age 21–30*]: the performance was quite beautiful, capturing the
pathetic humor, weakness, sadness, passivity, inexorability, unpre-
dictability, and the strange attractiveness of human life (*B.A.C.*);
I didn't realise from reading the play that it was funny (*K.A.*); the
actors played to the audience, who, much to my annoyance, made
noises throughout. Playing Gogo as a queen was unnecessary
(*S.A.B.S.*); the sense of being lost without time is saddening. The
humour merely emphasises this (*J.P.A.*); being an American alone
in London, I feel very akin to them. . . I feel suspended in time,
because there's nothing here which reflects my existence (*M.P.*); I
didn't like the totally flippant way most lines were delivered
(*J.A.C.*); boredom is a terrible thing, as is cruelty and selfishness
(*H.S.*); I feel the hopelessness and futility of life (*A.H.*); a very
professional performance of a difficult play. The difficulty arises
since it is the overall impression that matters and individual
speeches (obviously often absurd) are not *by themselves* important.
Whether the correct overall impression comes out without prior
reading of the play is debatable [this spectactor had not read it],
but this is the fault of the playwright and not the performance
(*J.G.C.*); the performance itself I considered excellent, but my
initial reactions to the play itself were rather strange in as much
that prior to this performance the only contact I'd had with *Godot*
was to read it (two years ago). I was aware of a totally different
reaction to the dialogue and the situation. Upon reading the play
I considered it a very moving and tragically symbolic work – not
completely devoid of comedy but certainly not comic to the same
extent as the staged version. In that respect I thought myself a
little disappointed – possibly shocked out of a set reaction (*P.N.M.*);
the play in my way of thinking had no real deep-rooted intellec-
tualism, but concerns two people waiting for something. The whole
of mankind is either waiting for something or someone or running
away from something or someone. If a play has no clear concise
answer or theme, like *Godot*, people always try to read too much
into it (*G.E.H.*); an amazing play; I feel dazed and inarticulate
(*R.I.C.C.*); it made me think that perhaps we cannot be very certain
that we are really experiencing something at those times when we

think we are (because our senses tell us we are), particularly because, the next day, what have we but our own memories, those of others (as reliable as Estragon's), and a few little clues that might just as well mislead us as help us. . . (*D.J.B.*); struck by the pathos of man's inhumanity to man and how amusing it is (*S.G.*); it shows the plight of humanity from loneliness and boredom (*C.M.L.H.*); I feel that I can understand *Godot* better now than when I first saw it. The clowning of itself does not help understand but it passes the time. Go down Cable St any lunch hour, Drury Lane any Saturday morning (11 a.m.) and meet Gogo or meet me sometimes (*G.R.D.*); I feel that the rest of the audience came between me and my total involvement in the play. I think that the view of life which I infer from the play (an interpretation which is influenced by my own personality) is one which many of the spectators do not have, and so there was a conflict between my own reactions and those of other people (*M.I.S.B.*); [finally in this age group there is this reaction which, although political rather than personal, is worth recording as an addition to critics' identification of Pozzo with De Gaulle, USA, Stalin, etc., etc!:] it seems that imperialist society (Pozzo) finally allows minorities to speak (Lucky) then turns on them when they exhibit themselves as men. This seems to directly show the problems of Rhodesia and other nations where minorities are oppressed (*C.C.C.*).

[*Age 31–40*]: realised hopelessness of many ventures and time being wasted (*J.F.B.*); extremely enjoyable and much more understandable than I had thought would be the case. I was surprised that many of the audience seemed to find it much funnier than I did. I found it disturbing that many seemed to find Lucky laughable. My main impression was of pathos (*J.B.*).

[*Age over 40*]: confusion and feeling of sad loneliness (*E.S.*).

[*No age given*]: I feel that these problems must be very common among people as I realised that most of their [the characters'] worries, needs, reactions are mine (—); like most modern plays, the comedy comes through only on the stage for me. The printed page only seems to invoke rumination on dark, 'existential', clever things. But maybe that was the phase I was going through, late in my teens, when I first read *Godot*. Both reactions have been valid – the soul-searching and the laughter. Good old Beckett! (*I.D.H.S.*); brilliant dialogue, themes of time plus dreams, truth, puts his finger very neatly on internal wilderness or . . . (*J.G.*); performance? (*S.A.S.*); very bright, energetic performance. I could imagine a subtler one, but this one communicated a lot very directly (*C.R.G.B.*); I found

I could identify *real* people in the characters themselves, that is, not particularly large types of people but individuals (—); reflection of man's interaction with man, while waiting for the inevitable, *i.e.* the end of existence. V and E demonstrate (1) ambivalence of man's wish for the company of another *vs* wish to be alone, (2) perpetual need to relieve the boredom of life by diversion/amusement. L and P reflect man's need to overcome feelings of insecurity by either excessive control/mastery over others or allowing oneself to be totally dominated. Inability to face up to reality satirically demonstrated by blindness and deafness. Final scene demonstrates continued conflict – to put an end to this inevitable waiting oneself (*i.e.* suicide), or wait until the chop comes from the hand of? (—).

(*b*) (GODOT, *Nottingham Playhouse*)

[*Age 20 or under*]: There is despair and yet eternal hope; blind acceptance and deep questioning, I want to read the play again, think about it, maybe see more of life before I understand it (*S.E.M.*); I would have enjoyed the performance more than I did if I had not previously read and studied the book (*J.E.*); I feel that there is no hope, I feel lost, that there is no reason for the existence of life, but I do not feel at all depressed. I feel almost dazed – so much seems to have been packed into the last three hours that it will take a long time to think about all of it (*A.M.M.*); I didn't really understand it, but found it very amusing in parts and somewhat depressing in others (*R.C.*); mingled reactions – laughter, aesthetic pleasure; ultimately deeply moving, even disturbing (*N.C.N.*); very moving, particularly Act II. Struck a note of deep tragedy, the characters seemed devoid of hope, the comedy futile (*E.C.*).

[*Age 21–30*]: this production got more humour out of the play. If you have nothing, you can only cry or laugh; the latter is best. Saturday-night, middle-income audiences can't respond to this play (*T.A.*); the most complete theatrical experience I have had (*B.W.M.S.*); I found that my reaction was not the same as that of many of the people in the audience. There were certain 'comic' situations at which the audience laughed – I found that these situations were disturbing and even pathetic in the fact that Vladimir and Estragon were so visibly wasting time and incapable of doing anything concrete in order to pass the time away (*G.L.C.*); the play gives tremendous insight into the boredom and futility of life. One can see so much of one's own existence in that of Didi and Gogo. If offers no 'spiritual joy', but to be depressed by it would be to become depressed by existence itself – and that would make living too difficult (*P.R.W.B.*); not depressed despite depressing subject. Surprising amount of humour relieved the tragedy (*D.P.B.*); depressing feeling of loneliness (*H.R.D.*); during the performance I remember laughing – sometimes it was a 'natural' reaction to something genuinely funny, but sometimes I felt I had laughed as a nervous reaction to an uncomfortable development (of the situation on the stage) – which makes one feel awkward for a few moments after. I'm not suggesting this is regrettable – it's just an indication to me that the play (or Beckett) is presenting me with awkward situations which I sometimes identify with. The recognition of these situations (through the medium of theatre) jolts me and causes me to attempt to face them and look at them anew! (*V.J.R.* – this spectator had not read or seen *Godot* before).

[*Age 31–40*): this particular production was so mixed – one star plus several *actors* – that it failed to quite reach me as an integrated vision of a universe devoid of value (which is what I take it to be about) (*D.C.*); it gives tremendous scope to the imagination because one can read all kinds of interpretations into the characters, their behaviour and conversations (*J.M.C.*); I felt the humour brought out by the two tramps alleviated the suspense (in the audience) of the endless 'waiting for Godot' (*A.R.D.*).

(*Age over 40*]: at interval, felt play to be clever but tedious. Second half more gripping. Sorry not to have been given an 'answer' but guess Beckett's totally negative (on purpose?) (*C.M.G.*); it was so clear this time. Either I'm wiser or this production is much better than when [*Godot*] first done years ago (*J.B.*); courage and hope are worth hanging on to, even in the face of enormous doubts (*N.T.*); the play is a challenge to actors, and its success depends a great deal on their interpretation. In this production they succeeded (*C.E.R.*); the arrogant assumption that man's existence must have a definable reason always makes me sad (*D.R.P.*); very amusing antics that never robbed one of the pathos of the situation (*J.D.*).

(*c*) (ENDGAME, *Young Vic*)

[*Age 20 or under*]: total depression, gratitude for the life I lead. I will fight boredom and being in a rut more now (*C.M.B.*); much more depressed by this than by *Godot*. Much more pessimistic and the humour is cruder (*J.H.*)

[*Age 21–30*]: at many points very possible to anticipate (*R.J.A.*); moments of feeling that I understand what Beckett is saying then a general feeling of confusion. I enjoyed *Endgame* as much as *Godot* –

but feel it was more fragmentary and obscure (K.A.); impressed with production and acting, but bewildered and thoughtful about play. Feel happier than when I went in to see play. Interested, not bored (*E.J.L.*); SHATTERINGLY GOOD, much better than before (*A.A.N.*); I am afraid I feel rather tired and dreary – looking back I can't say my attention wandered, but I was bored and sleepy. Then perhaps this was the intention – but after a long day's work I'm not sure I'm ready for plays that tell me life is dreary, bitter and pointless. It grabbed me and I shan't forget it but I didn't enjoy it and I feel no better for seeing it (*M.M.K.*); of course this sheet assumes some sort of neutrality concerning other factors, notably:

actors' performance;
immediate environment;
other external factors.

I have not yet found a playwright or group of actors who could completely shut these out from my point of view as an *audience* – partaking is different for me. Musicians come closer to this because of the force of their impact on the environment. I think Beckett is an advanced playwright in terms of the above point of view. However, his intellectual involvement becomes a negative factor at times where it stretches comprehension to the point of substituting your own thoughts and concerns for those which are directly a result of the dialogue – to this extent its effect may then become more a product of the above factors (performance, environment, etc.) (*B.H.L.*); easier on the surface to understand than *Godot*, but I think that the obvious interpretation of 'the end of the world' (after the nuclear bomb) etc. is probably not the right one. I am sure there is a 'deeper' meaning that I don't really understand. I was amused during the first half, but when the humour died out, it began to worry me, as the characters seemed to be running round in an unending circle of events, repeating themselves over and over again. I felt that the play was very poignant. The four characters were in desperate need of one another, if they had only admitted it. None of them understood what was happening (*J.M.C.* – who had neither read nor seen the play before); I felt how much one is dependent on other people for one's very existence. Also, that life and death can be very much self-chosen (Hamm allows himself to die at the end of the play). Life for the majority of mankind is extremely limited and boring – and even wealth (which Hamm has) cannot necessarily give one freedom to escape from this. Most importantly, I felt how much one is responsible for other people and the quality of their life (*R.M.B.H.* – who had not seen or read the play before); appalling 'theatre' which fails to engage my enthusiasm therefore interest. A slight embarrassment at what are clearly gifted (and certainly hard-working) performers putting so much in and (for me) failing to give anything to the audience. I find it depressing that the "intellectual snobbery' of audiences, actors and directors succeeds in retaining a place for this kind of intentionally vague non-entertainment. If this is 'theatre' then may it soon drop dead (*W.E.O.*); I still believe Beckett is very good literature but it is extremely difficult to translate him into good theatre, and this play in particular: of four characters, three are immobile. I don't think this primary difficulty was overcome in this performance (*C.S.*).

[*Age 31–40*]: basically unfulfilled – no real relation to the context of reality (*R.T.E.*); I was rather fearing a depressing evening but found that for me the impact was at the level of the rational and thought-provoking rather than the emotional. I was touched and moved by some of the 'memories of reality' – Beckett's spare yet fine use of language. I felt rather annoyed at times by the audience laughter – maybe because I was thinking mostly of sad undertones in the philosophy of the play (*A.L.*); I know a little about Beckett's work already, so I suppose that my reaction was conditioned by my expectations of seeing another howl of How Pointless it All Is. I got it. Parts I found moving, but in others I couldn't help feeling that the identical performance in another context (say a satiric show) could have been a parody of itself. I am sorry to sound so flippant, but I find Beckett's philosophy, which he follows so honestly to its logical conclusion, so repulsive that I don't sympathise with him much. Man without God is logically like this – except Beckett doesn't acknowledge that there is happiness at all in material life; but, if so, I can't see why Beckett bothers to write (*D.T.*).

[*Age over 40*]: perhaps I should watch it in the morning because then I have more flexible mental resources. Now, I am exhausted by the continuous tension of attempted understanding. But, at the end, I have only transferred emotion. Dear Samuel, is that what you intended. . . ? (*D.B.*); although I had seen the play before, I was extremely impressed with this production. A wonderfully heightened atmosphere in the Studio, the actors compelling the audience to concentrate. The tenderness of Nagg for Nell touched me profoundly. In *Endgame* Beckett has touched on the great sadness of non-communication and I thought all the actors conveyed this with great feeling (*G.McL.*).

PART II

Question 6. 'How did the play affect your view of human existence?'

(a) GODOT, *Young Vic*

[*Age 20 or under*]: In a way it made me more aware than ever of man's hopelessness. People never take the chance when it's there. They constantly complain, but never actually do anything themselves to improve whatever they happen to be complaining about (*S.V.*); the play has highlighted, to me, the routine aspect of human existence (*A.R.M.*); it clarified any vague feelings I had about the purpose of existence and gave me much firmer ideas with which to contrast my own philosophy (*C.M.B.*); the play suggested that the human race is composed of opposing parts. Man does not improve with time and the only relief from his situation is the existence of an external force. Before seeing the play I thought that man was improving his state by science etc. (*S.-J.A.*); it destroyed several illusions I had had, and heightened my somewhat vague impression of the mundanity and aimlessness which rule life as we know it, to a certain extent (*P.A.H.*)

[*Age 21–30*]: it confirmed my conviction that it is rather futile to wait for something like 'Godot' or to pin one's hope on a 'call from above' (*F.L.* – who also added the following comment on Q.II,7: 'The play was pessimistic as far as its contents are concerned. In my opinion, however, it was optimistic at the same time, because the wonderful creative impact of the play left me elated and happy, rather than dejected'); overall feel more pessimistic than before, more conscious of man's inhumanity to man (*J.G.*); the play has not changed any of my views. On the contrary, I interpreted *Godot* according to my pre-existing views (*P.G.F.S.*).

[*Age 31–40*]: I find *Godot* compassionate, it stimulates convergent thinking and is *demanding* of feeling, and although I remain outside the situation it touches all I try and comprehend of humour, pathos, confusion, fallibility, need for other human beings, courage. I see it diagrammatically as a series of concentric circles, each of which represents our experience at different levels. Sometimes an experience moves us in a whorl – perhaps *Godot* moves one nearer the essential middle (*A.G.*).

[*No age given*]: *Godot* is a witty play, full of lines which both sum up and parody its content. These lines tend to become part of one's imaginative stock, *e.g.*.., 'blaming on his boots the faults of his feet', 'People are bloody ignorant apes', 'Nobody comes, nobody goes, it's awful', 'They give birth astride of a grave, *etc.*'. Examples from other sources might be 'Whan maistrie comth, the god of love anon/Beteth hise winges, and farewell! he is gon', 'I can resist anything except temptation', 'The more Pooh looked, the more Piglet wasn't there', 'These fragments I have shored against my ruin', etc. This is not meant to be a frivolous answer. I think the quality I have tried to describe is important, although not all important works have it (*R.D.F.*).

(b) (GODOT, *Nottingham Playhouse*)

[*Age 20 or under*]: it made me start thinking again about the purpose of life, the meaning of existence, particularly as a few days later I attended a religious service at which the two alternatives given by the speakers were a belief in Christ, or in meaninglessness (*S.E.M.*); the play affected my view of human existence in that it consolidated my opinion about life. We need a God, whether internally created by ourselves or not, to give our existence meaning (*N.C.N.*); before seeing *Godot* I tended to regard human existence as futile, the play has merely reinforced this idea (*E.C.*).

[*Age 21–30*]: the play is so absolutely relevant it crystallises a great deal of the fundamental questions about existence (*B.W.M.S.*); their whole existence was centred around something that never came. In the same way the play made me think that perhaps the existence of most humans is waiting for something to come along and that life is made up of many disappointments, since we are continually seeking the ideal (*G.L.C.*); *Godot* provided an emotional link between philosophical discussion of the meaning of existence, and my understanding of the immediate human situation in relation to emotional growth, communication, and the need for relationships (*H.R.D.*).

[*Age 31–40*]: it confirmed my view of life, *i.e.* that life does not have values, purpose, or meaning *inherent* in it; it unfolds, it evolves, under its own biological 'momentum'. As animals with memories, self-awareness, and foreknowledge of our inevitable deaths, we are forever trying to jump outside our time-bound and inherently purposeless (or end-less) existence. Of course we always fail; and of course we take a certain short-lived pleasure in the cunning with which we avoid facing up to these inevitabilities (*D.C.*).

[*Age over 40*]: the play intensified my characteristic depression but also intensified my determination to thrash rather than drift (*J.B.*).

(*c*) (ENDGAME, *Young Vic*)

[*Age 20 or under*]: it affected my view of human existence in that it made me more aware of the fact that I am not the only person who feels lost and bewildered about the reason for their existence. It also made me see that far too much unhappiness and selfishness is caused by people who are desperately searching for an explanation and proof of their existence, which is something they will never find until they die. They would be far happier if they stopped trying to explain their existence and tried to enjoy it while it is still theirs. Nevertheless I now feel more tolerant of other people who are disturbed, and who become totally egocentric (*L.G.*).

Question 18. 'Why did performance have a deeper effect than reading?'

(*a*) (GODOT, *Young Vic*)

[*20 or under*]: to read a play can be an awful bore. If you see the play acted it comes to life – it contains emotion, and words said convey so much more meaning than words read because a lot depends on *how* things are said. I always enjoy a play more if I see it before I read it. After all, plays are meant to be plays – a form of entertainment – reading a play is always rather second-rate to me (*E.A.M.*); it has far more impact. It isn't only words that make a play but the facial expressions, gestures, moments of complete silence, etc.; of course, it is possible to imagine all this from reading the play and the stage directions, but to actually see it and to be involved in it from outside has far more effect. Some plays, from the way they have been written, seem to call for reading rather than acting, e.g. Shaw (*C.A.H.*); performance made meaning clearer. The added comedy was very effective. Well acted, especially Lucky, whose importance I did not really realise when I read the play. Being near the characters gave a feeling of being involved and therefore it was far easier to appreciate the play than if one were reading it (*S.V.*); the actual performance of the play is more effective because one is presented with the characters before you – real people in effect, whereas in reading one sees the characters solely as images, and all images tend to be blurred. Similarly, one achieves more the routine of human existence, comparing Act I with Act II – and seeing the great similarities, than one does when reading the play. Also, the language of the play is far more fluent when being performed than when read, because of the difficult nature of the language used (*A.R.M.*); it is the overall effect that's important and to search for deep meanings in phrases would at first be useless without knowing more about the overall message of the play. Reactions and appearance of the characters also make it more effective – obviously, or Beckett would have written a novel or a poem, not a play. Performance is the medium that artist has designed his work for (*J.H.*); you can rarely read a play without any interruption whatsoever, therefore some of the impact is lost. With this play, a lot of the humour would be lost if it was read, and one might think the two tramps were slightly cardboard figures, but seen as flesh and blood, especially in the 'intimate' atmosphere of the Young Vic (*C.M.B.*); when reading a play, the thoughts are your own and you have the power to shut the book or read without feeling. When watching real people involved in a tragedy it is impossible to remain uninvolved and ideas are introduced which might not have occurred in reading (*S.-J.A.*); when reading a play, part of your attention must be given to conjuring up visual images (*J.P.*); the play was more effective when performed because the actors' expressions and movements helped to make the script comprehensible. Originally I read the play, but did not get nearly as much out of it (*P.A.H.*); performance has a deeper effect because the dialogue in Beckett is quite sparse. The play is much more than what is printed in the script. . . . Also in the play there is the audience – one is thrown into the mood, one senses the reactions of other people. There is no time to muse, to be distracted, to close the book. One becomes part of the play going on around one. *Godot* becomes not a story, but life (*C.G.*).

[*Age 21–30*]: it's a boring play to read. The performance brings out the comic elements in it (*P.J.C.*); the quality of the actors' performance effects my enjoyment more so than with any other type of play. The actor's voice, timing and expression are all-important. The long silences are necessary to accentuate typical mundane expressions (*M.M.*); the answer to this question is as true of this play as of any other similar play. I am a very poor reader and find it very difficult to read a play (or anything very long, i.e. 50+pages) at a sitting. Because this play is 'difficult' it is helpful to be provided with clues (even if the other answers show I haven't taken them up) which help one to an interpretation – it's very much harder to work out the clues for oneself when one is reading. The short time-scale of the production helps to see the whole in perspective (*G.R.D.*); an emotional reaction to a play (as opposed to an intellectual one) is more strongly induced by seeing a performance than by reading it. . . . However, I think that reaction to a play must be to another person's interpretation of it, as it is enacted by virtue of the form (*M.I.S.B.*); one should see the play first, then read it, for in reading the man in the audience can remember scenes from the play and at the same time study the words. He now has a basis for comparison. He can see how the director interpreted a scene, and he can read the text and derive his own interpretations (*R.A.*); the spontaneity of the performance and its freshness had a terrific impact on me (*H.S.*); the source of the effect that the play will have lies (or lay) in the mind of its author. A live performance, correctly interpreted (by people who have proved themselves better than most in so doing), will convey that original idea to the mind of an observer with a better *chance* of accuracy than that provided by the observer reading the play straight from the book. . . . This is my personal point of view and comes from an ordinary person. It might not be the viewpoint of a scholar, but then, to whom is the play directed, particularly in view of its subject-matter? (*D.J.B.*); dialogue written in this sort of style is easier to appreciate by ear than by eye (*J.B.*).

(b) (GODOT, *Nottingham Playhouse*)

[*Age 20 or under*]: I thought that the play was more effective when I read it. The performance appeared to be a bit of a let-down. I expected to really enjoy the play (*J.E.*); I think that the play needs to be read and thought about for a long time, then to be seen (*A.M.M.*); on reading it the comedy is more pronounced. When it is acted out in front of you it is more pathetic and tragic. People laugh at it to keep themselves from crying and screaming (*E.C.*).

Age 21–30]: the most striking benefits of this particular performance for me from the point of view of amplifying (or perhaps recalling) the text lay in the distinction in character between Estragon and Vladimir. In this and in other ways dramatic performance will always increase one's knowledge of the text (*B.W.M.S.*); the actors can act so much better than I can read (*P.R.W.B.*); the high standard of the performance greatly increased the degree of involvement, because one was able to experience and accept the intense emotions it aroused simultaneously to others. This resulted, in my own experience, in a desire to withdraw, mingled with a feeling of communication [communion?] (*H.R.D.*).

[*Age 31–40*] unless one *sees* Vladimir and Estragon forcing themselves to think up little bits of byplay or *sees* punctilio, the former can seem (verbally) too repetitive and the latter a mere caricature (*D.C.*); when reading it so much of the sense of timing is lost (*A.R.D.*).

[*Age over 40*]: reading would not have emphasised the essential tediousness of time passing. I thought perhaps the whole tedium of life depicted in the play was to make one realise how wonderfully different is 'real' life in contrast when one returns to it again after the play (*C.M.G.*); reading clarifies detail, but a good performance tends to unify the play and crystallise the meaning. I saw *Godot* several years ago and it struck me then as completely futile and boring. (It may have been a poor production or it may possibly have been that I was not in the right frame of mind.) This time I tried to go with a completely open mind and found it a most entertaining *study* in futility – quite a different thing (*M.H.G.*); when I read the play a year or so ago I thought it a lot of 'hot air' or 'rubbish'. But this performance made me see the play in a completely different way. . . . The affection between Vladimir and Estragon needs to be seen, for it heightens the pathos and seems the essence of the play to me, for those two characters have between them the essence of life – affection, love or what you will (*C.E.R.*); reading left me with a very positive and moving impression. However, the performance in question heightened the impact (pauses, humour) (*J.D.*).

(*c*) (ENDGAME, *Young Vic*)

[*Age 20 or under*]: on the stage awareness of the claustrophobic atmosphere is increased. The dialogue of *Endgame* does not lend itself to very easy reading, it is far easier to appreciate the text and not become bored with it when also seeing physical action (*L.G.*); you miss a lot of what Beckett is saying if you just see it once (*M.M.*).

[*Age 21–30*]: *if* the performance is of such a high standard as the Young Vic's the play is more effective when acted (*G.M.H.*); the impact is much greater when one sees a play in the heightened atmosphere of a theatre, and there is also the reaction of the audience to the performance. Visual impact+speech+action are much more effective than the passive act of reading a script (*R.M.B.H.*); I wasn't emotionally involved when reading it, whereas in this well-acted performance I was moved tremendously (*P.H.*).

Very many more made the point that since a play is written to be performed, the best way to experience it is in the theatre. This was not really the point of the question; many of the answers quoted above attempt to analyse the additional effectiveness of the theatrical experience, rather than taking it for granted.

Appendix III *A Beckett – Ionesco Chronology*

This brief guide lists the major dramatic works according to date of *first performance* in any language. Unless otherwise indicated Beckett's plays are published in the UK by Faber and Faber, in the USA by Grove Press; Ionesco's plays are published in the UK by Calder & Boyars, in the USA by Grove Press. For more detailed bibliographical information the reader is referred to *Samuel Beckett: His Works and his Critics*, Raymond Federman and John Fletcher (University of California Press, 1970), and *Ionesco: a study of his plays*, Richard Coe (Methuen, 1971).

	BECKETT	IONESCO
1950		11 May: *La Cantatrice chauve* (Paris) [UK: *The Bald Prima-Donna;* US: *The Bald Soprano*].
1951		20 Feb.: *La Leçon* (Paris) [*The Lesson*].
1952		22 Apr.: *Les Chaises* (Paris) [*The Chairs*].
1953	4 Jan.: *En attendant Godot* (Paris) [*Waiting for Godot*].	26 Feb.: *Victimes du devoir* (Paris) [*Victims of Duty*]. 8 Aug.: *Sept petits sketches* (*Paris*) incl. *Maid to marry, The Leader,* and *The Motor-Show.*
1954		14 Apr.: *Amédée ou Comment s'en débarrasser* (Paris) [*Amédée or How to Get Rid of It*].
1955		15 Oct.: *Jacques ou la soumission* (Paris) [*Jacques or Obedience*]. 21 Nov.: *Le nouveau Locataire* (Helsinki, in Swedish; Paris, 1957) [*The New Tenant*].
1956		20 Feb.: *L'Impromptu de l'Alma, ou le Caméléon du berger* (Paris)

1956 – continued

1957 13 Jan.: *All That Fall* (BBC).
1 Apr.: *Fin de partie* and *Acte sans paroles I* (London) [*Endgame* and *Act without Words I*].

1958 28 Oct.: *Krapp's Last Tape* (London).

1959 24 June: *Embers* (BBC).

1961 17 Sept.: *Happy Days* (New York).

1962 July: *Act without Words II* (London).

13 Nov.: *Words and Music* (BBC).

1963 13 Oct.: *Cascando* (radio play for voice and music) (ORTF).

1964

1966 28 Feb.: *Va et vient* (Paris) [*Come and Go*].
4 July: *Eh Joe* (BBC TV)

1969 16 June: *Breath* (New York).

1970

[*Improvisation, or The Shepherd's Chameleon*].

23 June.: *L'Avenir est dans les oeufs, ou il faut tout pour faire un monde* (Paris) [*The Future is in Eggs, or It Takes All Sorts to Make a World*].

27 Feb.: *Tueur sans gages* (Paris) [*The Killer*].
31 Oct.: *Rhinoceros* (Düsseldorf, in German; Paris, 1960).

16 Apr.: *Délire à deux . . . tant qu'on veut* (Paris) [*Frenzy for two . . . and the same to you*].
15 Dec.: *Le Roi se meurt* (Paris) [*Exit the King*].
15 Dec.: *Le Piéton de l'Air* (Düsseldorf, in German; Paris, 1963) [*A Stroll in the Air*].

30 Dec.: *La Soif et la faim* (Düsseldorf, in German; Paris, 1966) [*Hunger and Thirst*].
28 Feb.: *La Lacune* (Paris). (This and *Va et vient* were part of the *Spectacle Beckett-Ionesco-Pinget* given at the Odéon-Théâtre de France, directed by Barrault.)

24 Jan.: *Jeux de massacre* (Düsseldorf, in German under title of *Der Triumph des Todes;* Paris, 11 Sept. 1970).

K

Appendix IV   *A Select Reading List of Critical Works*

A. GENERAL

Abel, Lionel, *Metatheatre* (New York, 1963).
Bentley, Eric, *The Playwright as Thinker: A Study of Drama in Modern Times* (New York, 1955); *The Life of the Drama* (London, 1966).
Brustein, Robert, *The Theatre of Revolt* (Boston, 1962).
Chiari, Joseph, *Landmarks of Contemporary Drama* (London, 1965).
Cohn, Ruby, *Currents in Contemporary Drama* (Bloomington and London, 1969).
Dort, Bernard, *Théâtre public* (Paris, 1967).
Esslin, Martin, *The Theatre of the Absurd* (Garden City, N.Y., 1961; London, 1962); *Brief Chronicles* (London, 1970).
Grossvogel, D. I., *20th Century French Drama* (New York, 1958); *Four Playwrights and a Postscript* (Ithaca, N.Y., 1962).
Hinchliffe, A. P., *The Absurd* (London, 1969).
Kitchen, Laurence, *Mid-Century Drama* (London, 1960).
Kerr, Walter, *Tragedy and Comedy* (London, 1967).
Pronko, L. C., *Avant-Garde: The Experimental Theatre in France* (Berkeley, 1964).
Shank, Theodore, *The Art of Dramatic Art* (Belmont, 1969).
Styan, J. L., *The Dark Comedy* (Cambridge, 1962).
Surer, P., *Le Théâtre français contemporain* (Paris, 1964).
Williams, Raymond, *Modern Tragedy* (London, 1966).

B. ON BECKETT'S PLAYS

Barnard, G. C., *Samuel Beckett: A New Approach* (London, 1970).
Coe, Richard N., *Samuel Beckett* (London, 1964).
Cohn, Ruby, *Samuel Beckett: The Comic Gamut* (New Jersey, 1962; (ed.) *Casebook on Waiting for Godot* (New York, 1967).
Duckworth, Colin, Variorum edition of *En attendant Godot* (with critical introduction in English) (London, 1966).

Esslin, Martin (ed.), *Samuel Beckett: A Collection of Critical Essays* (New Jersey, 1965).

Fletcher, John, *Samuel Beckett's Art* (London, 1967).

Hayman, Ronald, *Samuel Beckett* (London, 1968).

Mélèse, Pierre, *Samuel Beckett* (Coll. Théâtre de tous les temps) (Paris, 1966).

Modern Drama: 'Beckett' number, ed. Ruby Cohn (vol. 9, No. 3, December 1966).

Onimus, Jean, *Beckett* (Desclée de Brouwer, Paris, 1968).

Reid, Alec, *All I Can Manage, More Than I Could* (Dublin, 1968).

Robinson, Michael, *The Long Sonata of the Dead* (London, 1969).

Scott N. A., *Samuel Beckett* (London and New York, 1965).

C. ON IONESCO'S PLAYS

Abastado, Claude, *Ionesco* (Bordas, Paris, 1971).

Benmussa, Simone, *Ionesco* (Paris, 1966).

Coe, Richard N, *Ionesco: A Study of his plays* (new, revised, and enlarged edn, London, 1971).

Donnard, Jean-Hervé, *Ionesco dramaturge, ou l'artisan et le démon* (Paris, 1967).

Jacobsen, J. and Mueller, W. R., *Ionesco and Genet: Playwrights of Silence* (New York, 1968).

Knowles, Dorothy, 'Ionesco's Rhinoceroses', *Drama* (London), Autumn 1960, pp. 35–9: 'Ionesco and the Mechanisms of Language', *Modern Drama*, Vol. 5, No. 1, May 1962, pp. 7–10.

Sénart, Philippe, *Ionesco* (Paris, 1962).

Wulbern, J. H., *Brecht and Ionesco* (Urbana, Chicago, London, 1971).

Index of Themes and Ideas

abreaction 94

absurd, concept of 23, 27, 28, 36–7, 102, 109, 111

Absurd, Theatre of 53

action: choice of 66; dramatic 50, 52; objective validity of 46

agoraphobia 63

alienation effect 53

anguish: articulation of 29; cause of, in Samuel Beckett's characters 51, 62–3, 65, 76, 104; death as source of 23, 27–8, 34, 40, 42, 73; empathic transmission of 41, 107; metaphysical 89

anti-heroes 110

anxiety, transferred 70

archetypal: dreams 85; image of *quadrature circuli* 90; image of uterus 89; motif of engulfment 88; myths 85; qualities/structure of plays of Samuel Beckett and Ionesco 85, 93, 106

audience/spectator(s): empathic participation/percipient 41–2, 44–5, 51, 69, 71, 85, 93, 105; introjective function of 49; Ionesco on 41; response as act of creation/as part of creative process 45–6, 51, 60, 106; reaction survey(s) 20, 53, 78, 98–104, 106, 111, 116–43; relation to plays 14, 19–20, 44, 49, 69, 93–5, 98; and transmission of neurotic disturbance 57; as voyeur 47

autotherapy, plays as 93

avant-garde theatre 59, 103, 110

Backward Id theory 92–3

birth/reproduction, Samuel Beckett's concept of 35, 38, 72, 110

boredom/futility 70, 74; simulation of 84

catharsis 94–6, 99, 105, 115n.

child, schizophrenic *see* schizophrenic; *see also* birth

choice, freedom of 66

Christ 64, 80; *see also* Cross; God

Christianity and *Waiting for Godot* 18, 111

circus music 53

classicism 110

cliché: Samuel Beckett's use of 35; Ionesco's use of 40

clinical approach to literary criticism 44, 68

comedy, metaphysical 36, 93, 105

comic: counterpoint 75; and pathetic, interplay in Samuel Beckett 78; sense of, in *Godot* 55, 86; *see also* humour; jokes; laughter

communication, need for 21

compassion in Samuel Beckett's plays 48, 104, 109

confessional element 57

conflict within the author, theatre as 86, 92

consciousness 66; deep level of 107, 111; imprisonment of 22; longing for release from 39–40; parallel levels of 60; void at root of 109

construction, play as 85; *see also* structural; structure(s)

creation: act of, audience's part in *see* audience; and direction 106; artistic 57

creative process in Ionesco and Samuel Beckett, 93

critic(s): effect of Samuel Beckett's plays on 20, 45, 52; function of 98; psycho- 44, 89; *see also* psychoanalysis and criticism

Cross, the 81, 90

cruelty, theatre of 44, 86

cyclic events and circularity of time 87

death: in Samuel Beckett's work 34–5, 72; experience of 25–7, 41; fear of (in Ionesco) 28–30, 34, 38–41, 106; and laughter 79; *see also* mortality

death-instinct 29

deity, archetypal image of 90; *see also* God

demiurge 91

'demystifier', Samuel Beckett as 39
destruction, man's predilection for 28
deus absconditus 91
diachronic quality 71, 74
directing, as stage of creative act 106;
  see also production
double bind 66–7
dream(s): archetypal 85; in relation to
  Ionesco's work 60; *see also* nightmares
dreamlike flying 32, 60; *see also* weightlessness

empathic participation/percipient *see*
  audience
endlessness: in *Lessness* 92; terror of
  62–3, 65
engulfment, motif of 33, 88
eternal/every day, oscillation 69
eternity 22, 27, 87; terror of 62
evil, sense of, in *Godot* 86–7
existence: embryonic 89; problem of
  30, 33, 64; reality/validity of 23–4
existential: exploration, Samuel Beckett's 106; fear of non-being 39;
  position of ontological insecurity 63;
  problems 56; reconstruction of basic
  human situation, *Godot* as 84
extinction 48

fantasy(-ies): author's exploration of
  46; creative, and neurosis 89; inconsequential, in Ionesco 41, 106;
  private, in drama 43; schizophrenic,
  in plays 55
Flood, the 88
foetal urge 89

God 80–1, 90–1, 102, 104, 111; denial
  of his existence 65; and existential
  act 51; Samuel Beckett's view of 32,
  37, 77, 91; Ionesco on 41; *see also*
  Christ; deity; *deus*
guilt of having been born 36

harmony and aesthetic pleasure 93
heaven and earth, imbalance of 89
hell 87
help, acceptance of 64–5
hermeneutics, structural 85, 93, 105
hesitation-doodles 86
humanisation of speculations on exis-
  tence/death 24

humanity/human condition 24, 27–8,
  38, 74; *see also* man
humour, in Samuel Beckett's works 73,
  109; *see also* comedy; comic; jokes;
  laughter

identification with Samuel Beckett's
  characters 53–4
identity: continuation/resurrection of
  22; sense of 63–4; sense of, in Samuel
  Beckett 48; *see also* personality; self
imagination: motivated by concern 34;
  subconscious 85
imaginative horizons, enlargement of
  73
imprisonment: in *Endgame* 48; in finite
  time 87, 104; of human consciousness 22; within one's life-span 21;
  within the universe 20–1, 23, 104
indignation in Samuel Beckett 34, 38
individual and society, dichotomy between 104
infinity 21–2, 87; *see also* timelessness
insecurity, ontological 63, 71, 93
inside and outside, relation between 64,
  87
integration search for 27
intensity: poetic/dramatic, of Samuel
  Beckett 84; and primordial images
  89; of reaction 71
isolation: of stage from spectator 109;
  state of 74

joke(s), existence as 36–7; *see also*
  comedy; comic; humour; laughter
joker, Ionesco as 59

language: as dead 27; disintegration of
  47; of drama 25; playing with 74;
  theatrical, Samuel Beckett's 71
laughter: in Samuel Beckett's plays 78,
  80–1; three types of 77; *see also*
  comedy; comic; humour; joke(s)
levitation 32; *see also* dreamlike flying;
  weightlessness
life as existential illusion 35
limbo 77
loneliness in face of death 40
love: creative, Ionesco on 38; transcends
  death 39
lyricism in Samuel Beckett's work 84

malignant force, existence of 86
man: Heidegger on 46; as mortal 23–4; nothingness of 103–4; wholeness of 90–2; *see also* humanity; woman
mandala(s) 89–91, 105, 115n.
massification, fear of 104
mental state, dramatisation of 57, 61
metaphor, Samuel Beckett's plays as 84
mobility, need for 21
mortality: escape from 32; Ionesco on 73, 93; in literature 23, 25, 27; plays 38; problem of 59; *see also* death
mud, Ionesco on interpretation of 89
myths, archetypal 85, 89

néant see void; *see also* non-being; nothingness
neurosis(-es) of author 44; and creative fantasy 89
neurotic disturbance: in drama 69; in Samuel Beckett's plays 56–7
nightmares, dramatisation of 44, 60, 68; *see also* dream(s)
nihilism 73, 107
non-being: fear of 71; off the stage 47, 49
"not being" of characters 58
nothingness: of man/the self 103–4; of space 62; *see also* void
novels 28

ontological: insecurity 63, 71, 93; prison 109, 114n.
opposites, fusing of 109
optimism 108

participation, audience *see* audience
participation mystique 89
participatory democracy 106
personal element in Arrabal 43
personalistic plays 69, 89
personality: centre of 90; sense of, in Ionesco's work 59; *see also* identity; self
pessimism in drama 24, 43, 107
philolophy(-ers) 24, 75, 107
physical deterioration 29
plot(s) 52
poetic power in Samuel Beckett's drama 84
political solutions 43, 104
politicians, optimism of 108

primitive, instinctual state 86
primordial image(s) 88–9
production, Samuel Beckett's interest in 52; *see also* directing
psyche: four functions of 92; split in (Didi/Gogo) 67; (Hamm/Clov) 64; (Pozzo/Lucky) 67, 92; unification of 91
psychic: disturbance and dreams 60; exploration, Samuel Beckett's plays as 65; problem, expression of 69
psychoanalysis and criticism 57, 93; *see also* critic(s), psycho-
psychoanalysts 66
psychoanalytical theory, Jungian 39
psychodrama(s) 29, 58–9, 90, 103
psychodynamic relation of playwright and spectator 44
psychopathic characters 69
psychotherapy 103
punishment, life as 36
purgatory 33, 87

reality, representation of 47
reality sense 58, 65; Ionesco on 58–9
'reciprocal interrogation' 45
redemptive force of tragedy 106
religion 91; *see also* Christ; God
repetition 62, 88, 109
revolt 27
role-playing 51; and reality sense 58
rotunda 89, 91

schizophrenia 64–5, 70; and Samuel Beckett's plays 54–5
schizophrenic: child 62; split 67
scientists 107–8
self: creation of spurious 61; and death 30; divided 85 (*see also* psyche, split); dramatic exploration of 42, 44–5, 61, 109; -healing 90; -knowledge, as function and effect of drama 14, 45, 103; -knowledge in Ionesco 39; nothingness of 103; revelation of identity of 58
selfhood: search for 27; sense of, and memory 59; validity of, at death 26; *see also* identity; personality
shapelessness: v. shape in Samuel Beckett's works 62, 89; of universe 27, 62

silence: in Samuel Beckett's plays 81–3; as end-factor in Samuel Beckett's plays 32; in *The Killer* 27; of professional critical audience 52
social change 43
society and individual, dichotomy between 104
space: as limitation 21; terror of endlessness in 62
spectator(s) *see* audience
spiritual strivings/spirituality 27, 106
structural: balance 92; function of silence 82; hermeneutics 85, 93, 105
structure(s): circularity/repetitiveness of, in *Godot* 87–8; dramatic 69; and subconscious effect 89; of subconscious imagination 85; symmetry of, in *Godot* 92; verbal/word- 84, 89–90; *see also* language
subconscious: and *Godot* manuscript 86; structuring 70
suffering: Samuel Beckett on 103, 104; death as end of 79
synchronic effects 71

tension: between play and audience 98; in Samuel Beckett's works 71, 73, 87; /release, alternation 69, 78; of silences 83
théâtre panique 106
therapeutic function/value of drama 20, 45, 58, 103
time: cyclical theory of 33; imprisonment in 87, 104; as limitation 21; mythical v. historical 88; preoccupation with passage of 88; problem of 30, 33; unlimited/indeterminate, terror of 62
timelessness, ideal state of 38; *see also* infinity
tragedy: function of 57; in Ionesco 31
tragic, Beckett as 23
transience of life 34
tree: in *Godot* 66, 79–80, 90; no escape from 114n.; as symbol of deity 90
two thieves 78, 80

unconscious: collective 89; depths 85; sinking of libido into 88
universe: infinite 23; shapelessness of 27, 62
uterus, archetypal images of 89

vas hermeticum 91
vision, poetic 84
visionary plays 69, 89
void/*néant*: and consciousness 109; Samuel Beckett's beings exist in 51; of nothingness 32; silence as 83; *see also* non-being, nothingness

weightlessness, Ionesco on 89, 106; *see also* dreamlike flying
wholeness: alienation from 87; of man 90–2
will to live 40
woman 28; relationship to man 38; role of 115n.
womb *see* uterus
world-view: insecurity as 63; of spectator 49

'zero degree' of theatre 45

Index of Names and Titles

Abel, Lionel 16
All that Fall 34
Arrabal, Fernando 43, 54, 86
Artaud, Antonin 86, 94
Auerbach, Erich 109

Barnard, G. C. 61, 67–8, 92
Barrault, Jean-Louis 110
Barrucand, Dominique 94
Bastide, François-Régis 41
Bentley, Eric 58
Bergson, Henri 69
Blake, William 67, 92
Blin, Roger 50
Bossuet, Bishop 75
Brine, Adrian 53, 102
Brook, Peter 96

Chairs, The (Ionesco) 49–50
Coe, Richard 109

Dante 33–4
Dépeupleur, Le 21
Devine, George 16
Diderot, Denis 68, 107
Dort, Bernard 45–6, 95–6, 103
Dukore, Bernard 92–3
Dunlop, Frank 98

Eliade, Mircea 85
Eliot, T. S. 84
Emery, Jack 83
Endgame 38, 61, 64, 88
Epicureans 25
Esslin, Martin 20, 53, 84, 93–4, 98, 101
Exit the King (Ionesco) 29–31, 76
Eyre, S. R. 108, 110

Freud, Sigmund 60, 62, 68–9
Fry, Christopher 84

Gabor, Dennis 108
Genet, Jean 54, 86
Gielgud, John 84

Giraudoux, Jean 25, 110

Happy Days 28, 32–3, 36–7, 74, 96
Heidegger, Martin 42, 46, 75
Herbert, George 75
Holbrook, David 107–9
Huis close (Sartre) 25
Hunt, Hugh 68

James, Peter 51, 99
Jeux de Massacre (Ionesco) 38–41, 54, 73
Jung, Carl Gustav 44, 56–7, 60, 68–9, 85, 89–92

Kafka, Franz 63
Kaufman, Wolfe 54
Kenner, Hugh 18
Kerr, Walter 110
Killer, The (Ionesco) 27–9
Koestler, Arthur 71, 96

Lahr, Bert 66
Laing, R. D. 63
Lamartine, Alphonse de 76–8
Lesser, Simon 57
Leyburn, Ellen Douglass 95
Living Theatre 48
Lynch, Alfred 67

McCann, Donal 66, 83
McGowran, Jack 81, 83
Mathieu, Michel 45
Mercadet (Balzac) 18
Merleau-Ponty 25
Metman, Eva 85
Middlemass, Frank 81
Mihályi, Gábor 94–5
Moreno, Jacob Levy 58, 90

No Why (John Whiting) 35
Norwid, Cyprian 82

Obey, André 88
O'Toole, Peter 20, 66, 80, 83, 98, 101–2

Page, Anthony 16
Peterkiewicz, Jerzy 82
Pinter, Harold 83, 95
Pirandello 48
Portmann, Adolf 107–8, 110

Reid, Alec 94, 101–2
Renaud, Madeleine 37, 54, 96–7
Richard II 23
Richardson, Ralph 84
Robbe-Grillet, Alain 46–7
Robinson, Michael 34
Rosenblatt, L. M. 94
Rosenkrantz and Guildenstern are Dead
  (Tom Stoppard) 26

Saroyan, William 13
Sarraute, Claude 28
Sartre, Jean-Paul 25, 58
Schneider, Alan 53, 80
Sèchehaye, M. A. 64
Seneca 25
Shakespeare, William 63
Shank, Theodore 45
Shaw, George Bernard 34

Shaw, Robert 103
Stoics 25
Storey, David 84
Stravinsky, Igor 62
Strindberg, August 72
Stroll in the Air, A (Ionesco) 32

Trilling, Lionel 63
Tynan, Kenneth 14, 43, 67

Ulysses (James Joyce) 56, 85
Unnamable, The 21

Victims of Duty (Ionesco) 58–9

Waiting for Godot 34–6, 64, 74, 76, 78–
  82, 84, 86–7, 90; Beckett's discussion
  16–17, 68; and convicts in San
  Quentin 20; impact in mid-fifties 15;
  and schizophrenia 54–5
Wardle, Irving 83
Weales, Gerald 13
Williams, Raymond 110

Young Vic 51–3